# Rising Signs

*What Your Ascendant Sign Reveals
about Your Personality Type and More*

© Copyright 2022 - All rights reserved.

The content contained within this book may not be reproduced, duplicated, or transmitted without direct written permission from the author or the publisher.

Under no circumstances will any blame or legal responsibility be held against the publisher, or author, for any damages, reparation, or monetary loss due to the information contained within this book, either directly or indirectly.

**Legal Notice:**

This book is copyright protected. It is only for personal use. You cannot amend, distribute, sell, use, quote, or paraphrase any part, or the content within this book, without the consent of the author or publisher.

**Disclaimer Notice:**

Please note the information contained within this document is for educational and entertainment purposes only. All effort has been executed to present accurate, up-to-date, reliable, complete information. No warranties of any kind are declared or implied. Readers acknowledge that the author is not engaging in the rendering of legal, financial, medical, or professional advice. The content within this book has been derived from various sources. Please consult a licensed professional before attempting any techniques outlined in this book.

By reading this document, the reader agrees that under no circumstances is the author responsible for any losses, direct or indirect, that are incurred as a result of the use of the information contained within this document, including, but not limited to, errors, omissions, or inaccuracies.

# Free Bonus from Silvia Hill available for limited time

Hi Spirituality Lovers!

My name is Silvia Hill, and first off, I want to THANK YOU for reading my book.

Now you have a chance to join my exclusive spirituality email list so you can get the ebooks below for free as well as the potential to get more spirituality ebooks for free! Simply click the link below to join.

P.S. Remember that it's 100% free to join the list.

## ~~$27~~ FREE BONUSES

- 9 Types of Spirit Guides and How to Connect to Them
- How to Develop Your Intuition: 7 Secrets for Psychic Development and Tarot Reading
- Tarot Reading Secrets for Love, Career, and General Messages

## Access your free bonuses here
https://livetolearn.lpages.co/rising-signs-paperback/

# Table of Contents

INTRODUCTION ................................................................................... 1
CHAPTER 1: INTRODUCING THE RISING SIGN ..................................... 3
CHAPTER 2: IDENTIFYING YOUR RISING SIGN ................................... 12
CHAPTER 3: UNDERSTANDING YOUR RISING SIGN ........................... 24
CHAPTER 4: ARIES RISING AND TAURUS RISING ............................... 36
CHAPTER 5: GEMINI RISING AND CANCER RISING ........................... 46
CHAPTER 6: LEO RISING AND VIRGO RISING ..................................... 55
CHAPTER 7: LIBRA RISING AND SCORPIO RISING ............................. 65
CHAPTER 8: SAGITTARIUS RISING AND CAPRICORN RISING ........... 75
CHAPTER 9: AQUARIUS RISING AND PISCES RISING ......................... 85
CHAPTER 10: A GUIDE TO EMBRACE YOUR RISING SIGN ................. 94
CONCLUSION ................................................................................... 104
HERE'S ANOTHER BOOK BY SILVIA HILL THAT YOU MIGHT LIKE ................................................................................................. 105
FREE BONUS FROM SILVIA HILL AVAILABLE FOR LIMITED TIME ................................................................................................. 106
REFERENCES ................................................................................... 107

# Introduction

Whether you're new to astrology or have been interested in astrological signs for a while, it's common to be confused regarding which zodiac signs affect you. Whether you believe it or not, your zodiac sign is not the only astrological entity affecting your life. Every single one of the planets, zodiacs, and celestial bodies affects you. Out of these, one of the most misunderstood placements is regarding the ascendant or the rising sign and how it impacts your life. If you're one of those who don't understand this, then this book is the perfect guide to help you learn how the ascendant works.

Understanding how the rising sign works paves the way to understanding the truth about yourself. The rising sign highlights the most important themes and patterns of your life and, thus, holds the key to understanding your natal chart. Therefore, it's essential that you clearly understand what the ascendant entails and that you are also able to identify your rising sign. After all, the rising sign establishes which planet is the chart ruler of your natal chart.

So, whether you want to be able to interpret your personal natal chart or help a friend understand their rising sign and zodiacs, this book will provide an in-depth description of each rising sign. Each of these comes with specific personality traits and mannerisms when approaching every challenge, difficulty, or situation. Understanding what motivates these approaches can help you understand an individual's mental psyche and behavior. Their rising sign and ruling planet explain much about their nature and why they act the way they do.

As a bonus, we have included an extra chapter on how you can embrace your rising sign. None of us has any control over when we're born, so we don't get to choose our ascendants and ruling planets. And while some people have no trouble accepting themselves for who they are, others find it very challenging to be happy with their true selves. The best way to deal with this is to first understand everything about your ascendant and then work toward accepting your sign and the traits that come along with it.

The placement of your ascendant is extremely sensitive, and understanding it is essential to understanding the entire astrological significance of your ruling planet. Therefore, it's best to first learn about the importance of the rising sign on your birth chart and then get into detail about all the traits that come with it. Knowing the difference between the sun and moon signs and the rising signs, as many people often confuse these with each other, is also key to a greater overall understanding of your chart and character. So, read on to discover everything about the ascendant and your particular rising sign traits and life patterns.

# Chapter 1: Introducing the Rising Sign

An astrological birth chart holds the key to a unique cosmic signature based on the placement of planetary bodies, zodiac signs, and houses. At the time and place of your birth, your birth chart depicts the position of the planets, sun, stars, and moon. We can discover all sorts of things about ourselves and our place in the world within the structure of astronomy.

The rising, the moon, and the sun are the three main planetary points within the birth chart that define personalities. The sun sign is well known to most people, but the moon and rising signs are less familiar. Did you know that the question of birth signs is much more complex than simply stating a zodiac or star sign? We are not just one single zodiac aspect. We are talking about the entire universe and its changing planetary alignments. All planets, celestial bodies, and galactic coordinates occupied astrological signs when you were born, and each had a unique meaning. Introducing the Rising Sign, otherwise known as your Ascendant, is essential as it is one of astrology's most integral yet overlooked placements.

Even if you're aware of what your rising sign is, you may not be so sure of what it means for you. So, we're here to explain it, along with an insight into why you need it and how it differentiates from the sun and moon signs.

# The Signs in Astrology

In astrology, there are plenty of symbolic representations to go around. Each sign has its own unique set of symbols, which practitioners often use as identifiers during a reading. These symbols provide additional insight into various attributes and characteristics in a person's birth chart. But what do these signs mean, and how do they come into play? Let's take a look...

Most people are familiar with their sun sign, also known as their star sign. What does a rising sign mean?

The signs of the rising sun on the day you are born are known as your rising sign or Ascendant. It is a subtle but powerful indicator of your personality and character. Utilizing their power through knowledge can help explain the rising signs in Astrology, their traits, and their compatibility with other signs. Peering into the future and analyzing horoscopes has been an indispensable part of our lives for many centuries now. Every human being on this planet has a set of stars and planets that influence their actions, thoughts, speech, habits, and every other action they undertake during their lifetime. The study of these celestial bodies and their effect on human beings is known as Astrology. The zodiac plays a considerable role in this field, with each star having its own particular significance and impact on people who are born under its domain.

Your first breath occurred at the moment of a unique configuration of all the planets. And when you get your natal chart drawn up, you'll see the sky as it appeared at the exact time, date, and location of your birth. These charts are potent tools astrologers use to understand and pass on information and insight into personal opportunities, personality, timing, identity, motivation, and recurring themes throughout life.

The birth chart includes it, along with the moon and sun signs - the foundation of your character.

- The moon sign symbolizes the inner you
- The sun sign symbolizes your essence
- The rising sign represents the outer you

Your rising sign determines what people think of you when they see you for the first time. Your rising sign may also explain why people might perceive you as a fickle Aquarius despite you being a serious Virgo.

## The Rising Sign

Your rising sign reveals a great deal about your personality and outlook on life. A birth chart's angle determines the alignment of the zodiac wheel, and it depends on the time of your birth. Here's your chance to better understand this part of you!

It is also called the ascendant because it rises over the eastern horizon at the time of your birth. Despite appearing static to the naked eye, the scene overhead actually moves extremely quickly. Ascendant and rising sign placement is also very sensitive. You need to know your exact (not approximate) time of birth to calculate your rising sign.

This is one of the most important aspects of a birth chart, one of the most defining and representative aspects within you, and it expresses your natal energy. Your natal energy is your life trajectory and personality. It is also one of the most misunderstood angles in the birth chart. Because we tend to think of the ascendant as how we appear to people or how we look, it is a projection of ourselves. But the ascendant is so much more and affects more in the birth chart than merely your outward appearance. Using your rising sign can be a great way to understand others' energy and personalities and show the same enlightening aspects of yourself.

Knowing how and why your signs are the way they are will help you understand them better. By understanding another person's ascendant, you can better understand their energy, preferences, and outlook of that person. It's an excellent way to get a sense of their birth chart. As a result, you can use it to work on things you need to improve in yourself, and understanding someone's ascendant helps you to understand their outlook.

### How Does the Rising Sign Affect Who We Are?

So, a rising sign represents how you appear. You give an impression to others based on how you project yourself, how you look, and how you behave. This angle on the birth chart depicts the impressions we give out of ourselves and others. This makes it an exciting part of your birth chart to explore, to know who you are to other people. This is because the rising sign, the ascendant, is the first self-impression determining factor of the birth chart. Despite differences in the placement of the planets, the rising sign is the one that sets and calibrates the zodiac wheel in our chart.

The rising sign indicates which sign is on the horizon at the time of birth. It determines our houses and what signs rule over our houses. The house system is a study of its own and is covered in other books. We need to know that a person's astrology chart is divided into 12 houses, each representing a different side of their life. The ascendant position in a chart establishes house systems. The rising signifies who you are, what you look like, and the words you use as you enter the first house. In other words, it represents a person's character and exterior, which are the first things that are noticed in them.

This then completely changes the personality type, and as it changes each sign, it will trail through different degrees depending on the degree of your ascendant. Therefore nobody is the same. Because every second of every day, through the celestial planetary movements, there is a slight shift in degree. This is known as the zodiac wheel. So, if people are born even one second apart, they will have very different personalities.

In contrast to the sun sign, which represents your inner core, is the moon sign, which symbolizes your center. Thus, rising signs are the masks you wear to the world.

**Why Are Rising Signs Important?**

Rising signs are vital because they give us information about people's personalities, character traits, and future. These zodiacal positions directly impact your life and influence who you are as a person. They also give insight into how other people may perceive you. How you view the rising sign will tell you a lot about your self-image and self-perception, especially concerning matters of the heart. Rising signs are also linked to elements such as the sun, moon, and earth. Understanding these connections can help you better understand how their position impacts your life moving forward.

The subtleties and complexities of the change aspects of astrology and ascendants dictate our energies and what we hold true in our lives. It creates different archetypes in each of our lives.

Things like money, relationships, health, outlooks, and philosophies all have different houses (rising signs) ruling them. The ascendant determines our houses, and which sign rules over which house is a definitive aspect of understanding ourselves and other people.

# Rising Signs in Practice

By knowing how to read rising signs, we can get a better understanding of why it is necessary to know this part of the puzzle. As already mentioned, the rising sign in your birth chart represents the planets ascending on the Eastern horizon when you were born. So, we can decipher what others think of us and a person's gut-level and spontaneous reaction to things. For example, during a difficult situation, a Leo rising will end things with a tremendous impact, and everybody will know about it. In contrast, a Pisces rising will leave more quietly. It is an essential part when determining personality type.

Rising signs determine how to deal with difficulty and come out of the shadow.
https://pixabay.com/images/id-3151869/

Our rising sign determines how we deal with things in our lives, coming out of the shadows and hardships. Ascension and spirituality are popular concepts, and your ascendant will show you what that looks like and how it works.

# How the Rising Sign Is Different

Whenever people ask about your star sign, they're referring to your sun sign or where the sun was when you were born. With more people becoming interested in astrology, rising signs are also becoming better known. Due to the rapid changes in the horizon, it is essential to know your exact birth time when looking for your rising sign.

Astrologically speaking, the sun sign, the moon sign, and the rising sign are the three most important signs. By meeting someone's rising, sun, and moon signs at different life stages, you will learn more about their character.

Generally, sign discovery on a person will work like this:

- Your first discovery will be the rising sign, which acts as a social guardian
- A sun sign personality follows
- Then, when trust is gained, the moon sign will appear

As the exterior representation of who you are, your rising sign corresponds to your outer self, your sun corresponds to your core self, and your moon corresponds to your inner self. If you're ready to dive deeper into personal astrology, take a moment to learn about rising, moon, and sun signs.

# The Sun Sign

The sun sign is the premise of many horoscopes, so when someone asks you what your sign is, it is generally related to the sun sign. You can determine your sun sign based on birthday information.

Sun signs are honored in astrology for a good reason. The sun sign defines who we are, just as the universe is defined by the sun. Knowledge of your astrological natal chart is necessary because it represents intellect, identity, vitality, and spirituality.

Astrology has been practiced for thousands of years. Around 2,100 years ago, the Babylonians developed their own form of horoscopes, and astrology soon spread to the Mediterranean. As we know them today, horoscopes were first introduced in the 1700s by astrologist William Lilly. Reading horoscopes became mainstream in the 1930s when British astrologer R.H Naylor started publishing birth chart predictions for the royal family. Naylor simplified his readings by focusing on sun signs for readers curious about their own astrological forecasts.

### What Can We Learn from the Sun Sign?

You will inherit a set of character traits and qualities that will help you achieve what you desire in life based on your sun sign. Zodiac signs each have their own rulings that guide and influence the personalities of those born under that sign. For example, it is known that Mercury is the planet of communication, which governs the Virgo sign. Therefore, you'll probably find you have yet to meet a Virgo who doesn't have excellent communication skills and the ability to handle any situation.

In astrology, the sun sign represents our highest expression of self, so it's no surprise that it's given added importance. Sun signs represent how we present ourselves to the world and are associated with specific sides of our personality. In a chart, the sun's place can indicate how someone expresses themselves, whether that is creatively or verbally.

Although your sun sign, determined by the sun's position on the day you were born, may be an essential part of your identity, it is not always comprehensive. On the other hand, your rising sign offers a lot more. Knowing your rising sign symbolizes integrating all the elements of your life and chart.

## The Moon Sign

After the sun sign, the moon sign is regarded as the next critical influencer on your horoscope. Sun signs represent the ego, while moon signs represent the inner self.

A person's moon sign corresponds to the moon's position at the time of their birth. About two and a half days pass between the moon's visits to each zodiac sign. Because an individual's personality and emotions are greatly influenced by their moon sign, according to the astrological universe, moon signs provide an insight into the inner self. Those deepest desires, thoughts, and fears we keep hidden from others can be identified by understanding the moon sign.

### What Can We Learn from the Moon Sign?

The moon sign separates us from people who share sun signs in terms of personality traits and qualities. You may also find that this lunar sign balances out the extremes of the sun sign. Alternatively, you may have a deeper understanding of yourself and others when both the sun and moon belong to the same zodiac. Essentially, the lunar sign is a gateway to emotions, the subconscious mind, and the inner voice. You can uncover much more about your individual potential if you use it.

In astrology, the moon is associated with maternal influence. It represents basic reactions and habits hidden deep within us. It corners the subconscious side of our thoughts and feelings that may lay dormant even to ourselves. The moon sign governs our inner self, bringing our fragility, sensitivity, and deepest desires face-to-face.

Even though the sun and moon signs can predict specific characteristics of your personality, astrology isn't an exact science, and your astrological profile is made up of various factors. Your horoscope is most accurate when all the placements in your chart are acknowledged.

## The Rising Sign

One of the most crucial points in a natal chart is the rising sign since it governs the first house of the ruler chart (when you were born).

On a symbolic level, it represents the spot where the sun rises each day and the point at which the earth and sky meet. In the chart ruler, wherever the rising ascendant degree falls, it sets up the rising sign, which is the foundation for all the houses. Houses describe the areas of life where the alignments of the planets fall. This is why the rising sign of the incident is so vital because it sets the stage for the rest of the chart.

In reality, a chart is more than just your internal world; it is a map of your life. Don't consider it the most prominent facet of your personality. Aside from the fact that it incorporates both internal and external dynamics, it is also the most technically important point in the chart, not because it carries more than the other components but because it is crucial to where the other components end up.

Rising signs reflect our external characteristics, including appearance, immediate responses, relationships, and attitude. In other words, it represents the appearance and persona of the self. Your rising sign energy may lead you to dress or look differently than your moon or sun sign energy does. In addition to guarding our deepest selves, rising signs can be used to increase insight and help us adjust to new situations with new people.

# The Different Components of the Three Signs

To find out about anyone's signs, you must know the exact place, time, and date of birth. There can be many rising signs among people born on the same day, making things very interesting.

- The place of birth determines the moon sign
- The rising sign is determined by the time of birth
- The sun sign is determined by the date of birth

The ascendant, also known as the rising sign, is associated with our social personalities, so it is possible that if someone is guessing your sign, they may get your ascendant before your sun sign. This is because our rising sign encompasses the characteristics of our outward appearance.

You can't just say you're a Virgo since that would mean your personality is the same as everyone else born in Virgo season. The Virgo sun may land in the tenth house of achievement and public roles, making them more of a public figure instead of the stereotypical homebody Virgo personality you may read about online. In the next chapter, we will discuss houses in more detail.

Whether you're new to the three signs or new to the rising sign, knowing it can make all the difference between knowing someone and truly knowing them - or even yourself! This is because there is a lot more to a person than the typical sun-only signs can provide.

# Chapter 2: Identifying Your Rising Sign

The astrology birth chart has captured your imagination, so you have decided to explore it for yourself. There's a saying that postulates that we don't come with an instruction manual. Let's think again about that! We can understand our personality and path by looking at our astrology chart. Our horoscopes can provide insight into our everyday lives and help us make life changes based on the planets' movements. What is the formula for interpreting the movements and locations of planets? Why do the planets affect the zodiac signs, and what is the definition of a zodiac sign?

To be able to read a birth chart, also known as a natal chart or astrology chart, we need to first understand these questions. A birth chart shows where the planets were at the time of our birth. It also provides information about our preferences, aims, and character. A birth chart gives the reader significant insight into a person. In this chapter, we will discuss what a birth chart is and detail its crucial component of one. We will then go on to discuss how you can identify your rising sign using a birth chart.

# What Is an Astrology Birth Chart?

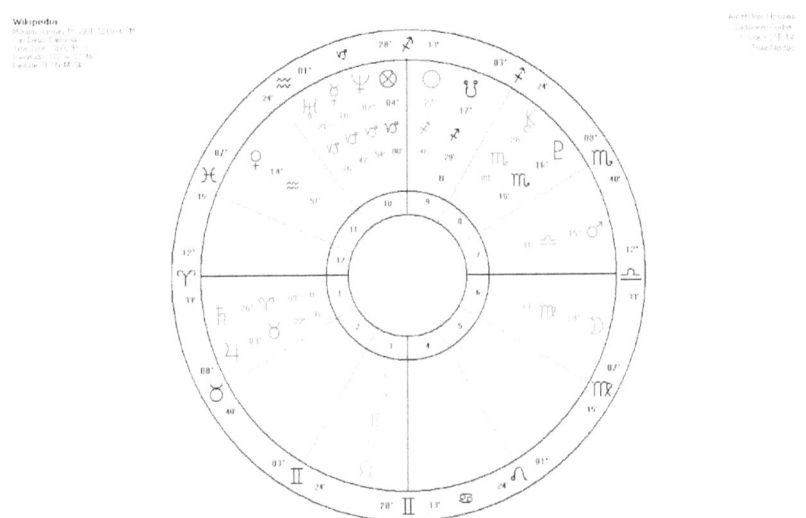

Sample Birth Chart.
*https://commons.wikimedia.org/wiki/File:Wikipedia_Sidereal_Birth_Chart.gif*

A birth chart may initially seem confusing, so let us explain what it is. It shows the sky at the exact moment and place when you were born as a two-dimensional map. It may seem like a confusing circle of glyphs and symbols when first laying eyes on one. There is no denying that a birth chart has its language. To decode it, you'll need patience, energy, and time. But once you become aware of what the symbols and lines mean, you'll soon ask for the birth information of everyone you know to discover their rising signs.

All of us have an astrological chart that identifies who we are. A birth chart can show you who you and others really are by calculating the astrological particulars of your birth. You can find out about your assets and liabilities and future growth prospects by analyzing your birth chart.

# What Does an Astrology Birth Chart Do?

Virgos are stoic, and Geminis are crazy. In general, these are some of the generalizations about the sun signs of the zodiac. The sun sign may be the most well-known feature of a birth chart, but there are other things to consider. Multiple planets are placed in 12 different houses in a birth chart. There is no such thing as a duplicate birth chart, just as there is no such thing as a duplicate person.

They reveal the positions of the planets at the time of birth for people, including insight into circumstances, connections, and ambitions. Even your pets will have their own specific astrology charts. For now, though, we will concentrate on yours.

Natal charts can give clues about someone's character and reveal significant events in their lives based on their placement of planets at birth. So, birth charts offer insight into our lives, pointing us in the right direction and helping us become the best version of ourselves. Most people see astrology as a way of participating in the world while shaping their futures rather than fate.

As an example, consider the following. If someone has a Uranus Pluto placement, they tend to never settle-always look for the next thing to try or place to go. But, if they understand that, it can help them to become more aware of what they're doing. You can gain insight into why you act the way you do in all aspects of your life by studying your birth chart. Positive behaviors are amplified, and negative behaviors are highlighted. Knowing why they happen will help you to prevent them from happening again.

## Why Is an Astrology Birth Chart Important?

A birth chart is a map of your life's purpose, just as a map shows rivers, directions, and places from our point of view. Similar to a map, it outlines precisely where things are, how to get there, and how things have evolved over time. Our very own life story is outlined, along with instructions on how to complete it. A birth chart can provide fascinating information about personality traits and behaviors. Using them can help you understand unseen areas and shape your perception. By doing so, we can improve ourselves and grow as individuals. The growth of your abilities can be improved by understanding your capabilities and shortcomings.

# Astrology Birth Charts: What We Can Learn

- Venus's zodiac signs and houses, as well as the sun and moon's
- Aspects or angles of the planets
- Each planet's house and zodiac sign
- There is a high concentration of energy if more than one planet is in a sign (stellium)
- Balance of the four elements (planets in fire, earth, water, and air signs)
- Balance of the chart (planets in changing, stable, or seasonal signs)
- Patterns of planets
- Jupiter is the planet of fortune, Saturn is the planet of preservation

Element and quality scores can be calculated by adding them together. If there is a deficit of one characteristic or dominance in another, we can learn to achieve equilibrium in our lives.

# Key Components of an Astrology Birth Chart

A birth chart takes the shape of a 360-degree circle. We position ourselves in the circle as if we were at its center instead of looking down from above. For example, West would be on the left, not on the right, and vice versa. As a result, the directions are flipped since we categorize it as if we are on the inside, looking out.

We discussed the sun sign in chapter one. Our horoscopes are based on this. The essence of who we are can be found in it. Further on, we discussed how we can know our emotional self through our moon sign and how we were raised. As an adult, it relates to our relationships and needs. At the time of our birth, we were born under a constellation, which gives us our rising sign, essentially indicating how we present ourselves to other people.

An astrology birth chart can provide insight into every facet of our existence.

# The Zodiac Signs

A birth chart consists of 12 sections around the outer rim. There will be a section that corresponds to your birth date. The Zodiac sign you were born under is determined by your birth date. Each sign of the Zodiac represents a distinctive personality.

- Capricorn (December 22- January 19)
- Sagittarius (November 22- December 21)
- Scorpio (October 23- November 21)
- Libra (September 23- October 22)
- Virgo (August 23- September 22)
- Leo (July 23- August 22)
- Cancer (June 21 - July 22)
- Gemini (May 21 - June 20)
- Taurus (April 20- May 20)
- Aries (March 21- April 19)
- Pisces (February 19- March 20)
- Aquarius (January 20- February 18)

You can read an astrology chart in more than one way, depending on how you read your Zodiac sign. A variety of factors influence the way your sign is read, so to do it successfully, understanding an astrology chart means putting all this knowledge together to get a true reading.

# The Houses

It is through horoscopes that we get a deeper understanding of astrology. The more we follow them, the more familiar we become with our birth charts and the more interested we become in them. Signs and planets are well known, but what on earth is a house?

Several areas of one's life are affected by a planet's energy, such as a person's relationships, profession, and sense of self. In the first house, the planet Mars represents individuality and motivation, and Aries governs this house. No matter what sign we are, we can use this method to define everything that makes us special.

Each celestial point, planet, or asteroid has its own house, and its placement provides valuable insight into our personal characteristics and how we live with the world around us. Different external and internal events are activated by the movement of the planets in the sky. Each house has its own sign.

There are 12 houses in the birth chart, just as there are 12 zodiac signs. For example, the 7th house of health symbolizes relationships, bonding, and romance, which corresponds with Cancer's energy, which is all about caring and emotions.

## The Twelve Houses

1. The self, body, temperament, appearance, and vitality (Ascendant level on the birth chart)
2. Possessions, resources, livelihood, and value
3. Community, relationships, communication, expression
4. Home, domesticity, foundations, and blood relationships (The Imum Coeli level (bottom) on the birth chart)
5. Creativity, children, pleasure, and romance
6. Routine, health, environment, well-being
7. Perspective, relationships, bonding, and romance (Descendant level on the birth chart)
8. Intensity, death, animalist, and desire
9. Philosophy, travel, exploration, curiosity, and open-mindedness
10. Image, appearance, achievement, and public roles (The Midheaven (top) level on the birth chart)
11. Support, friends, ideas, and joy
12. Inner self, emotions, secrets, and dreams

In case you still feel unclear about the difference between houses and signs, keep in mind that the moon passes through a sign in two to three days. During a 24-hour period, the Moon passes through every house in your birth chart. Every planet follows the same rule. The passage of Pluto through a house takes 24 hours but will take 12-31 years to pass through a sign.

# The Planets

You can interpret your reading based on the planets that pass through your chart's different houses. Different symbols represent the planets throughout the chart. Various energies are influenced by the placement of planets in your astrological chart that influences daily life.

- Neptune and Uranus combine to form Pluto. Two interlocking lines on either side form a female glyph
- In the form of an upside-down female glyph, two lines curve away from Uranus on either side
- An upside-down cross appears on Neptune with two lines curved skyward
- Mars represents males, while Venus represents females
- Two lines protrude from the top circle of Mercury, which is the female symbol
- The sun is represented by a circle with a dot in the center
- The moon is a small half-crescent moon shape
- The symbol for Jupiter is similar to the number four
- A symbol resembling five represents Saturn

Two types of planets exist within the birth chart: outer planets and personal planets.

The outer planets include Neptune, Jupiter, Uranus, Pluto, and Saturn.

- Neptune - spirituality, imagination, intuition, dreams
- Jupiter - philosophy, personal growth, wisdom, and luck
- Saturn - bonding, responsibilities, habits, and partnership
- Uranus - revolution, growth, learning, and change
- Pluto - passion, change, transformation, and evolution

Personal planets include mars, the sun, Venus, mercury, and the moon.

- The moon - intuition, privacy, memories, and reaction
- Mercury - communication, perception, information, and

efficiency
- The sun - identity, ego, truth, and individuality
- Venus - finances, comfort, enjoyment, and love
- Mars - passion, will, confidence, and energy

The planets play an important role in understanding the house's energy. For example, Venus within the fifth house is creative, while mercury within the first house is talkative.

The following information will help you better understand where things are on the birth chart.

### The Imum Coeli (IC)

Imum Coeli, or the IC, is situated in the Northern Hemisphere. This is the midnight of the chart, where our private lives are.

### The Midheaven (MC)

High noon on the chart corresponds to the midheaven in the Southern hemisphere. We are most visible in this part of the chart, where the Sun peaks in the sky.

### The Ascendant (AC)

The rising sign, or the sign of the Sun, in the birth chart is situated in the Eastern hemisphere (left side of the chart). When we are born, our ascendant degree represents us most intimately since it rises at the moment of our birth.

### The Descendant (DC)

The birth chart's setting (descending) sun is situated in the Western hemisphere. This point in the chart represents our close relationships.

The signs can help you better understand the chart now that you have examined the houses and the planets. Identify the house signs by looking at their ruling signs. You can then check which planets are in which houses and signs. Knowing your birth chart in this way will enrich your understanding. For example, a person with an Aries ascendant will be outspoken and confident, as Mercury is positioned here.

# How to Use an Astrology Birth Chart to Find Your Rising (Ascendant) Sign

Finding out your sun sign is easy enough to do these days. Simply unfold a newspaper, magazine, or Google search, and you'll find your horoscope anywhere. Finding the rising sign is going to be a little bit different. Remember, if you really want the best reading possible, we must do a few extra things first. When astrologers are doing a full birth chart, they'll often emphasize the ascendant or the rising sign more than the sun sign. And, in some instances, the importance of the rising sign is taking precedence more than it used to. Many new horoscope columns are written in many instances with the rising sign or the ascendant sign in mind rather than the sun sign.

For beginners, it is best to find out what sign their planets are in (e.g., are you a Virgo sun with a Capricorn moon?) and which house those planets fall in their birth chart.

Collecting information about your birth will be necessary to determine your rising sign. You can find an online rising sign calculator or visit an astronomer once you have this information. But there's nothing better than a good old DIY project. You may have learned all you know about astrology so far by yourself, so you may as well go one step further. Below you find all the information you need to discover your rising sign. Knowing your sign will help you understand what each planet represents when you interpret it. More of that is in chapter three!

### Your Date of Birth

Record your birth date, month, and year. This should already be obvious to you. Your birth certificate or parent can provide this information if you are unsure.

### Find Out About Your Time of Birth

It is important to know your time of birth to get an accurate answer because the rising sign changes every two hours.

But this can be tricky to do as not all of us know this detail of our birth. Sometimes, neither will our parents! Or they're not around for us to ask them. Ask some member of your family to give you a rough estimate. Your birth certificate may contain your date of birth. Knowing your precise time of birth will help you identify your rising sign. If possible, limit the time to at least two hours in the morning or evening.

### The Location of Your Birth

Taking into account your birth location will also be crucial, primarily because of time zone differences. If you're unsure of this information, ask your parents or check your birth certificate.

### Calculate the Time Difference

Time intervals are two hours apart on a rising sign chart. You may need to make some adjustments to certain areas since the sunrise could be after or before 5:30 when you were born. The chart may not work unless your date of birth is modified. Daylight savings time may also need to be considered.

- Subtract 1-2 hours from your birth time if the sunrise was earlier than 5:30
- You should add 1-2 hours to your birth time if the sunrise was much later than 5:30
- Deduct an hour from the time you were if your date of birth was during daylight saving time

A Farmer's Almanac, published during your birth year, is a great place to find this information.

### Find Your Sun Sign

Identifying your rising sign requires knowledge of your sun sign. Probably the most familiar Zodiac sign to you. Depending on what day you were born, your Sun sign can reveal a lot about your personality.

- Capricorn (December 22- January 19)
- Sagittarius (November 22- December 21)
- Scorpio (October 23- November 21)
- Libra (September 23- October 22)
- Virgo (August 23- September 22)
- Leo (July 23- August 22)
- Cancer (June 21 - July 22)
- Gemini (May 21 - June 20)

- Taurus (April 20- May 20)
- Aries (March 21- April 19)
- Pisces (February 19- March 20)
- Aquarius (January 20- February 18)

## Check out a Rising Sign Chart

On a rising sign chart, the twelve sun signs are displayed horizontally. Two-hour windows are displayed on the vertical axis. Navigate through the sun signs until you find yours. Calculating your birth time requires consideration of your local sunrise.

Below is a guide to your rising sign, the planets, zodiac signs, and houses so you can begin to piece together a complete chart.

| ZODIAC | GLYPH | PLANET | GLYPH | HOUSE |
|---|---|---|---|---|
| ARIES | ♈ | MARS | ♂ | 1ST |
| TAURUS | ♉ | VENUS | ♀ | 2ND |
| GEMINI | ♊ | MERCURY | ☿ | 3RD |
| CANCER | ♋ | MOON | ☽ | 4TH |
| LEO | ♌ | SUN | ☉ | 5TH |
| VIRGO | ♍ | MERCURY | ☿ | 6TH |
| LIBRA | ♎ | VENUS | ♀ | 7TH |
| SCORPIO | ♏ | PLUTO /MARS | ♇/♂ | 8TH |
| SAGITTARIUS | ♐ | JUPITER | ♃ | 9TH |

| CAPRICORN | ♑ | SATURN | ♄ | 10TH |
| AQUARIUS | ♒ | URANUS | ♅ | 11TH |
| PISCES | ♓ | NEPTUNE | ♆ | 12TH |

* Another glyph for Pluto is ♇

Astrology is complicated, and no matter how much we simplify our sun-rising horoscopes, learning our rising signs can still be quite complex. Nonetheless, with this comprehensive guide to discovering your rising sign, you will soon be well on your way to discovering more about yourself and others. There is more to understanding your rising signs in the next chapter.

# Chapter 3: Understanding Your Rising Sign

There is something frightening about identifying the unknown. This is why many people find identifying their rising sign challenging. The reason is that this aspect of astrology offers so much potential. So much of what we don't know about ourselves and others are hidden beneath the swirling glyphs, conflicting symbols, and confusing birth charts.

The best way to look at it is to remember that no matter how far back you go, through your adult life, angsty teenage years, carefree childhood, all the way back to your birth - your rising sign has always been there waiting for you to discover it. And why might that be? Knowing your rising sign can provide essential insight into who you are. There is no better place to delve deeply into the crevasses of who we really are than here.

Through chapter one, we went into the specifics of what constitutes a rising sign and why it is an essential aspect of astrology and the discovery of the self. In chapter two, we took a hopefully not-too-confusing look at a birth chart and how using one can help you identify your own rising sign. In this chapter, we will go through some of the more pertinent reasons why knowing your rising sign is necessary and what it can offer you in the long term. Then we'll take an exciting look at each specific rising sign and its characteristics.

# Benefits of Knowing Your Rising Sign

Astrology studies the position of the sun, moon, and planets in relation to one another in time and space. You can learn a great deal about yourself, your future life, and your place in the world by learning your rising sign. The rising signs are a treasure chest of knowledge. They reveal our hidden potential and uncover the secrets of our personality. They also give us insight into our compatibility with other signs in the birth chart. In fact, knowing your rising sign can be especially helpful because it offers you unique insights into your character. If you're interested in knowing more about your rising sign, we have all the details for you! Keep reading to learn about the benefits of knowing your rising sign.

### Discover the True Self

If you're aware of your rising sign and all that it means, you'll be less surprised by negative events in your life and more likely to deal with them positively. You'll also be better able to control your emotions and cope better with stress-inducing situations. In other words, our rising signs are like the guidebook of our entire lives, taking us through life's ups and downs, repeating cycles and themes. Eventually, making us aware of the patterns we will encounter in our lives.

### Better Reading

The problem with clinging to your sun sign as the only truth is that accurate sun sign horoscopes concentrate on the bigger picture. They are not tuned into the specifics. Reading for your rising sign will give your horoscopes a degree of accuracy you just can't find from sun signs alone. Sun sign predictions are almost always tailored to the current moment, which is why they aren't as accurate.

### Know Your Most Compatible Signs

If you know your rising sign, you can use it to find out which other signs are most compatible with you. This can help you decide who you should date and who you should avoid. For instance, if you have a Leo rising, you are most compatible with Cancer, Taurus, and Pisces signs. Similarly, if you have a Taurus rising, you are most compatible with Cancer, Pisces, and Virgo signs.

### The Bigger Picture

Undoubtedly, the rising sign plays a role in personal astrology. Besides influencing the way, we present ourselves to the world, it is also the basis for our entire birth chart (also known as the ascendant). Identifying your rising sign can help you understand your personality and become more aware of how others perceive you.

### Discover the Unknown

You can gain a deeper understanding of yourself and your inner intricacies by understanding your rising sign. You can also defend yourself against those who insist horoscopes are simply generalizations. Basing your reading on the rising sign is more reliable than the sun and moon signs we see in popular media today.

## Signs of the Rising (Ascendant)

Rising signs symbolize our personalities on a social level. It is the internal and external parts of ourselves. For example, understanding our rising sign helps us to understand the type of energy that drives life philosophy.

Having learned what rising signs are and how to locate yours, let's take a look at what each sign means. This is only a small glimpse of the zodiac rising signs, as a more in-depth feature will follow in the next few chapters.

The rising sign is one of the most helpful tools for understanding your personality. And knowing your rising sign can be especially helpful because it offers you unique insights into your character. Now that you know how your rising sign impacts your personality, you can use this knowledge to improve your life.

**NOTE:** As shallow as it may seem to characterize the physical appearance of rising signs, we have already established that the rising sign heavily influences an individual's appearance and outward manner. This can give us a better determining feature when interpreting the rising signs of others.

# Aries

March 21- April 19

**First Impressions**

Direct, confident, courageous, and strong.

**In the Chart**

Mars, the god of war, rules this planet. As the rising sign of the zodiac, Aries is a courageous fighter. You are the first fire sign of the zodiac, and you are intensely competitive in nature.

You lack tact and sensitivity and can be oblivious to others' needs, preferring to act self-sufficiently. You don't rely on social approval and reinforcement as much as others do and may act on impulse and with little forethought and precision.

You see yourself as a warrior and are eager to get into action as soon as possible. Consequently, Aries lacks patience and is careless with details.

**Characteristics**

Walking and moving swiftly is a hallmark feature of Aries rising. As well as prominent facial features, people born with this rising sign will have visible marks or scars. Aries' features are muscular, and they have an athletic physique.

# Taurus

April 20- May 20

**First Impressions**

Slow, attractive, sensual, and dependable.

**In the Chart**

As the most beloved goddess of love, and prosperity, Venus rules you. You can't help but be influenced by your sensual nature. This means you love to be active and creative with your hands.

Your Taurus rising means others view you as a rock of strength – dependable and consistent. You do things methodically, and you are extremely stubborn.

Despite appearing unfazed and collected, Taurus Rising reveals tremendous strength underneath. Due to your tenacity, you often prevail in disagreements. Your need for security is very strong, and you will not willingly change your present conditions unless forced to do so. Your home and job are all examples of tangible security.

**Characteristics**

In general, Taurus ascending relates to solidity, strength, and stability. Taurus rising personalities tend to weigh more because of their propensity to indulge. The most common physical attributes include broad shoulders and a stocky neck.

# Gemini

May 21 - June 20

**First Impressions**

Adaptable, social, intelligent, witty.

**In the Chart**

Mercury, the divine emissary, rules a Gemini. You are destined for immense success as a public speaker because you are charming and have excellent speaking skills. Having Gemini Rising in your sign also means you learn quickly but are susceptible to being easily distracted. You value variety and an active social life.

Others like interacting with you due to your humorous and intelligent nature. Your Gemini Rising makes you social, no matter how bad you feel. Because of this, you never appear somber.

Gemini risings are generally very social and witty.
https://www.pexels.com/photo/two-women-sitting-on-white-bench-1549280/

Serious people might find your behavior silly. By not taking life to heart, you keep a lighthearted attitude and a positive outlook. Gemini Rising is a restless sign, so consistency and reliability are not your strong suits. A slow pace makes you fidgety and nervous.

### Characteristics

People with Gemini rising signs are typically slim and seldom suffer from excess weight (unless they have a lot of Taurus or Cancer planets in their natal chart). They are usually always active and busy and don't enjoy staying still for long periods.

# Cancer

June 21 - July 22

### First Impressions

Emotional, Maternal, sensitive, nurturing.

### In the Chart

The intuitive moon rules cancer rising, so you appear kind. Having a deep desire for stability and connection, your friends and family are very important to you. Cancer Rising can make it challenging for you to accept new ideas or change from the familiar.

As someone who sees the world through a deeply individual viewpoint, it can be challenging to separate yourself from assumptions and stereotypes.

Your Cancer Rising gives you a caring personality, which shows itself in your dedication and support of the people you love. The ability to understand others' emotions makes you an empath. Given your caring and understanding nature, you are easily moved by others' distress.

### Characteristics

An individual with Cancer rising has a round, moon-shaped face. People with cancer also tend to gain weight, particularly on their hips. Legs are usually slim and short. Cancer Rising females are voluminous and curvy.

# Leo

July 23- August 22

**First Impressions**

Dramatic, playful, affectionate, creative.

**In the Chart**

Having the powerful sun as your ruling planet makes you destined for the spotlight if you have a flair for it. You are not shy or meek, and you rarely settle for having to play second fiddle. Having a Leo Rising makes you a leader by nature, not one to like to be dictated to.

Once you become friends with someone, you are extremely loyal and will do anything to make that person happy. You are kind and generous but don't want your generosity to go unnoticed; you always expect acknowledgment and appreciation.

When you have a Leo Rising, you always present the best possible face to the world, and you rarely show anyone when you are hurt or discouraged.

**Characteristics**

A Leo rising's hair is often their dominant feature and resembles a lion's mane. The head and facial features of these people are also strong. Having a regal disposition makes them a person who demands respect. Exaggerated mannerisms are characteristic of the Leo rising individual.

# Virgo

August 23- September 22

**First Impressions**

Innocent, humble, shy, helpful.

**In the Chart**

Mercury is the governing planet of Virgo risings, so they are inquisitive and expressive. As a protector of the zodiac, Virgo is extremely compassionate and will take a supporting role rather than the lead. You are modest, unobtrusive, and often quiet or shy.

When it comes to your own assessment of yourself, you are often very critical of yourself because of your humility; you strive for perfection. Often, when you doubt that you can live up to your own expectations, you won't try. You cannot express your spontaneous nature when you are not confident in yourself and your abilities. Yet, what you do, you do very well.

You deeply understand right and wrong due to your Virgo Rising. This unflappable disposition you display is evident to others. In spite of your kindness and caring, your lack of evident sympathy may prevent others from seeing your helpful qualities.

### Characteristics

The Virgo ascendant is associated with small, well-shaped facial features and fair, smooth skin. A Virgo rising has high nervous energy and is extremely sensitive. Presentable and well-groomed, this individual is usually well-dressed.

# Libra

September 23- October 22

### First Impressions

Indecisive, charming, peacemaker, graceful.

### In the Chart

Those born under Libra rising are flirty and ethereal, as Venus is Libra rising ruling planet. Conflicts are settled by finding common ground and similarities rather than focusing on the points of disagreement.

The Libra Rising expresses a strong desire for harmonious relationships and a willingness to be fair. Others' opinions easily influence young Libra risings because of your desire to be liked. Beauty is something you appreciate, and style and art are important to you in everything you do.

You are not an independent loner due to your Libra Rising; you enjoy being part of a close couple. The problem, though, is that you are prone to being overly dependent on your partner and struggle with developing an identity away from your relationship.

### Characteristics

Libras rising generally have a strong body, and the details of their face are distinct. When they reach middle age, however, their bodies get heavier. Their politeness and elegance are evident in their behavior.

# Scorpio

October 23- November 21

### First Impressions

Powerful, magnetic, mysterious, intense.

### In the Chart

Scorpio rising is ruled by Mars, the warrior, and Pluto, the ruling planet of the underworld. You have been through some things which made you guarded, especially if your chart includes other Scorpio influences. Despite your reserved demeanor, you are enthusiastic and driven.

Getting something requires quiet persistence and dedication. You don't fear danger or challenges because you're driven and enthusiastic.

Immediate intuition usually determines whether a reaction is favorable or unfavorable.

When you devote your emotional life to a relationship, you are deeply committed and dedicated, expecting loyalty in return. When someone has wronged you, you may respond with the same passion you once felt for them.

### Characteristics

One of the most distinguishing characteristics of Scorpio-rising individuals is their large, penetrating eyes. It is common for the skin to be shiny or sallow, with sharp features. The body usually has a lot of muscle, strength, and thickness. Lack of emotional expression is a typical characteristic of this personality type.

# Sagittarius

November 22- December 21

### First Impressions

Inspiring, cheerful, restless, and optimistic.

### In the Chart

Due to Jupiter's rule over Sagittarius, you consistently come out on top. A lot of the time, you dream about future possibilities and long for an experience more fulfilling than what you've had till now. Having your ascendant in Sagittarius, you like to have goals, but once you reach them, you move on.

This rising sign cannot withstand long-term confinement, and those close to you must respect your desire for independence.

There are times when you tend to exaggerate your excitement. Usually, you speak a lot, make lots of promises, and are pretty persuasive. A generous spirit permeates every aspect of your life.

### Characteristics

The most distinguishing features of a person are their facial roundness and a wide smile. Sagittarius risings are often awkward and clumsy. Their gestures are excessive and grandiose. An individual rising in Sagittarius is usually energetic but dislikes exercise and tends to overeat.

# Capricorn

December 22- January 19

### First Impressions

Determined, reserved, refined, and serious.

### In the Chart

You often approach the world with caution and reservation since you don't see it as do not a welcoming or secure place. You also have a wild side, which can be addictive to lovers. When young, you were already worldly and cynical.

In Capricorn Rising, you plan carefully to make the most impact with your activities. It takes dedication and persistence to achieve what you want. Some of the time, you don't ask for or need help from others.

When it comes to softer feelings, you dislike sentimentality. Instead of buying goods as fleeting indulgences, you invest in long-term, profitable investments. It is easy for you to live without because you are disciplined and self-controlled.

### Characteristics

Those with this rising sign tend to be lean and thin with bronze skin tones and sharp features. The rise of Capricorn can make this person seem distant.

## Aquarius

January 20- February 18

### First Impressions

Funny, creative, quirky, independent.

### In the Chart

As eccentric as you are, Uranus governs your horoscope. You are usually passionately dedicated to the community or philanthropic causes.

Fairness and equity are integral parts of Aquarius Rising's philosophy and outlook on life. The collective good matters as much to you as your own health.

In your interactions, you express impersonal goodwill. Many of your close relationships are based on shared ideals and principles rather than emotional ties, and you probably have many acquaintances but few close friends.

### Characteristics

There is usually a quickness and unpredictableness to their mannerisms and walk. The way they behave or dress leans towards the unusual, causing others to notice. Their features are distinct and aesthetically pleasing.

# Pisces

February 19- March 20

**First Impressions**

Sensitive, easygoing, impractical, imaginative.

**In the Chart**

You are ruled by the mysterious Neptune, which makes you alluring. This rising sign is compassionate and empathetic, with a positive perspective on life. Due to your distaste for confrontation and your timidity, you are likely to retreat in these situations.

In light of your Pisces Rising, your emotional balance and well-being need to spend time in quiet solitude in a peaceful environment. As a child, you frequently retreated into fantasy whenever life got too stressful or repetitive.

In Pisces Rising, people feel attracted to you because they sense your sympathetic nature. In many situations, Pisces rising will give to others even when they realize they are being exploited.

**Characteristics**

Individuals born under the Pisces rising sign are relatively small and well-proportioned. This sign is also associated with large, dreamy eyes and long, thick lashes on the ascendant. It is common for the feet and legs to be small and the arms and legs to be short. Usually, they speak softly and are shy.

This short breakdown of the rising signs should give you a better indication of what to look for on a birth chart. They are also quite useful when doing a reading. So, if you're interested in getting deeper into astrology, knowing the characteristics of the individual rising signs as they relate to a person can open up a wealth of knowledge.

Continue reading about the rising signs in the following chapter to discover even more.

# Chapter 4: Aries Rising and Taurus Rising

Now that you know what rising signs are, how they affect your personality, and how to identify yours, we'll discuss all the rising signs and their different personality traits in this part of the book. This chapter will focus on Aries rising and Taurus rising signs. We will discuss their mindsets and how a person born under these signs acts in the different areas of their lives like work, relationships, home, etc.

## Aries Rising Sign

**Aries Rising's Glyph**

Aries symbol.
*Bruce The Deus, CC BY-SA 4.0 <https://creativecommons.org/licenses/by-sa/4.0>, via Wikimedia Commons: https://commons.wikimedia.org/wiki/File:Deus_Aries.png*

### Aries Rising's Personality

Aries is a fire sign, and a person with Aries as their ascending sign can feel its fiery hotness in their attitude and even appearance. They are bold and hotheaded, which can be great qualities in most cases. However, at times, it can overwhelm those around them. Mars, the planet named after the god of war, is Aries's ruling planet, and Aries rising individuals can feel its impact on their personality. There is always a fire burning inside them that drives them to fight for what they want and always come out on top. These individuals are very energetic and enthusiastic, especially at social events. They are the life and soul of the party. Excited and passionate, everyone enjoys their lively conversation. However, boredom is their biggest enemy. They enjoy living an active life and like to have something to do.

As a result of the fiery energy inside of them, they don't like to sit on the sidelines, and they are always the first to take action. Impatient and impulsive, they would rather do something than sit and wait. However, they usually act before they think. Aries rising is a competitive sign; it is all or nothing with them. Although there is nothing wrong with being competitive in certain areas in life, they usually put themselves under a lot of pressure. Failure or losing is never an option.

People born under an Aries rising sign are independent individuals. The only person they rely on is themselves. Although there is nothing wrong with being independent, Aries can take it too far. They won't ask for help even when they need it the most. They usually depend on their inner strength and resilience. There is no denying that they can handle anything life throws at them, but they need to understand there is no shame in asking for help.

These individuals are straightforward and say it as it is. They don't care if people judge them or mistake them for being aggressive. They don't have ill intentions or want to hurt people; they are simply direct, honest, and blunt. They don't struggle with making decisions because they would rather act quickly than waste time thinking things over. However, some decisions require patience and time. As a result of their impatience, they usually don't finish projects and tend to flit from one project to the other.

They are brave risk-takers and are not concerned about consequences. The ambition of an Aries rising knows no bounds. They will do whatever it takes and will not stop until they reach their goals. At times, Aries rising can be selfish and insensitive to other people's feelings. However, they are kind and considerate when it comes to the people they care about. Aries rising individuals like to always look their best which is why they focus on their appearance. Their love for life is contagious, as is their passion and cheerful personality. Ruled by Mars, Aries rising usually has a short temper. However, they tend to cool down quickly and don't hold grudges.

**Aries Rising's Mindset**

We can summarize the Aries rising mindset in three words: new beginnings, emergence, and creativity. They are always in a hurry, and everything must happen right now. They happily venture out to the unknown because they see the advantages of taking risks. They never shy away from taking chances, especially on things most people would be reluctant to try.

**Aries Rising at Work**

When Aries rising walks into a room, everyone will notice them because they have a very strong presence. However, they are usually stable and grounding. They are critical thinkers and have strong work ethics, which help them advance in their careers. They don't let adversity get to them. If a plan doesn't work, they make the necessary adjustments and get the job done. Aries rising excel when working alone; however, they can work well with a team. They are born to lead, not to follow, which is why they usually seek leading and management positions at work. They are people who get the job done without making a fuss. These natural-born leaders excel in positions like CEOs or having their own businesses.

**Aries Rising in Relationships**

Because they are usually competitive and extremely focused on their work and projects, some people may think that an Aries rising person may not have time for relationships. However, it doesn't matter how busy they are. They find ways to show those closest to them that they are also important. They will never make the ones they care about feel like they don't matter. They are always there for them, especially when they need help. They aren't the type of people to change their priorities for others. However, if they make someone a top priority, then they must mean a tremendous amount to them. They aren't the type of people to be hung up on being in relationships. They will come through for the people they love, and if they make a promise or a plan, they will always keep them. Aries rising individuals are known to be loyal in a committed relationship.

### Aries Rising in Friendships

It doesn't matter if someone is a casual friend or a close friend; an Aries rising will always be supportive and help others with any problems they have. Even if a person simply needs someone to listen, an Aries rising will never get tired of listening to someone talk and will show them nothing but understanding. In fact, they are very empathetic individuals and will go above and beyond for the people they love. Their fighting nature doesn't only apply to them and their goals; they will also fight for people close to them. They are very private individuals that could be mistaken for being aloof. However, they are an "open book" with those close to them, like their partners and their best friends.

### Aries Rising in Love

When Aries rising is in love, they may not stop talking about their partners to others. They will want to show their loved ones off to the whole world because they know they are amazing and want others to see it too. They also want everyone else to know how important and special this person is to them. If there is an important event, whether professional or personal, they will ensure that their partner is by your side. That said, an Aries rising doesn't let their lives revolve around their partner, but they will still be there for them no matter what.

### Aries Rising at Home

Aries rising people love their family and include them in all special events. Their home is always open to their family members and the friends they consider family as well. Their home is their safe haven, so they make sure it is a comfortable and relaxing place where they can unwind after a long day at work.

# Taurus Rising Sign

## Taurus Rising's Glyph

Taurus symbol.
Bruce The Deus, CC BY-SA 4.0 <https://creativecommons.org/licenses/by-sa/4.0>, via Wikimedia Commons: https://commons.wikimedia.org/wiki/File:Deus_Taurus.png

## Taurus Rising's Personality

Taurus rising individuals are organized, hard-working, loyal, and patient. They have expensive tastes and an appreciation for the finer things in life. However, they can also be jealous, lazy, and stubborn. They are usually traditional individuals who prefer structure. They are productive and perfectionists. They avoid drama, which is why they are usually quiet in social situations. Whether it is their work or love life, they know exactly what they want and aren't afraid to go after it. They like the simple things in life and thrive in a quiet environment away from any tension or disturbance. For this reason, they always surround themselves with like-minded people who like to spread positivity. They are very stable and focused when it comes to achieving their goals.

Taurus rising individuals are loyal to a fault to their family and friends. They will always show up for the people they love offering unconditional love and support. People tend to gravitate toward them because of their agreeable and easy-going personalities. They are extremely consistent and rarely ever change their mind about something. It is almost impossible to sway or influence their opinions. However, this trait can have its disadvantages. They are stuck seeing things from one side and refuse to consider other perspectives. These individuals can be extremely rigid when it comes to their ideas, and they are resistant to change.

For this reason, Taurus rising individuals are considered very stubborn. If they set their mind to do something, nothing and no one can change it. Occasional stubbornness can be a good quality, but it can also have disadvantages as it prevents them from taking a different approach or going after new opportunities and experiences. These individuals are extremely focused and do things at their own pace. They don't appreciate being rushed or distracted. If they step out of their comfort zone, they will be surprised by what is out there.

Taurus rising individuals are extremely cautious with how they approach certain life situations. Unlike Aries' rising sign, they don't take risks or jump into things without thinking. They like to play it safe and weigh all their options first. However, not everyone appreciates this quality, especially these days when most people make decisions on the go. Although they are sensible individuals, others may see them as conservative or stand-offish. There is nothing wrong with being practical but remember to enjoy yourself every time.

Ruled by Venus, the planet of love and beauty, Taurus rising individuals are extremely sensual and feminine, although their practical and rigid personalities may make them seem otherwise. They know how to celebrate life's simplest pleasures like good food or hot sex. However, they may overindulge and value material possessions at times. They are also physically affectionate and love to greet the people they love with a warm hug. Another similarity they share with Aries is that they usually pay close attention to their appearance. They are creative, skilled, and disciplined, which makes them excel in whatever field they choose.

**Taurus Rising's Mindset**

Young Taurus rising individuals may seem older and more mature than their age because they have figured out a few things in life. As a result of having Venus as their ruling sign, they want to enjoy life and surround themselves with beautiful things. They like nice scents, a beautiful environment, and a serene atmosphere. When someone wants to win their heart, they can take them out into nature to see beautiful scenery like the mountains. In fact, they thrive in natural and quiet settings when they can be at peace and hate it if someone disturbs them. They would rather stay at home and watch movies than engage in someone's drama. They want to lead a peaceful and quiet life without any complications. However, some people may mistake them for being boring, but they are far from it. They just like to live a drama-free life and don't concern themselves with small matters. In fact, they can be the life and soul of the party if they can have interesting and fun conversations with others.

### Taurus Rising at Work

Taurus-rising individuals thrive when they are part of a community which is why they do well when working in a team. However, if someone disagrees with them, their stubborn and headstrong personality takes over. They are very creative individuals and enjoy sharing their ideas with other people. If someone has a different idea, they will happily listen to it. They may even experiment with new things but eventually, they will go back to their familiar tried and tested. They are very curious about people, especially in the work environment. They are interested in discovering the motivation behind other people's actions and what drives them to act a certain way. If they find someone acting differently, they won't pass judgment. They will give advice when necessary or challenge people to help them see things from a different perspective.

### Taurus Rising in Relationships

Taurus rising individuals can be jealous and possessive in relationships and find it difficult to end things. They are very loyal when they are in love, but they can also be very intense. These individuals are very sensual and thrive in stable relationships. Their calmness hides their very passionate nature. They are usually very private within relationships. However, they don't intend any malice; they simply value their privacy. These individuals would rather have light-hearted conversations than engaging in heart-to-heart or serious conversations. They don't like showing their vulnerable side because they want to appear charming in front of their loved ones.

Things are different when they start trusting someone, as they find it a lot easier to get close to them. However, they will still not open up or share their innermost feelings. They are great listeners and make other people feel comfortable enough to open up to them. Thanks to their loyal nature, these people's secrets are usually kept safe. They prefer to listen than to talk as this can help them learn more about the people in their lives.

### Taurus Rising in Friendship

As a result of their private nature, they may confuse their friends at first. They usually don't share anything with them, making it frustrating to be a Taurus rising's friend at first. However, once a person gains their trust, they will reveal their truest self. However, they will still keep a part of themselves hidden from the rest of the world.

### Taurus Rising in Love

Taurus rising individuals make great partners when they are in love. In fact, love is the only thing that can make them venture out of their comfort zone because they are willing to do anything for their loved ones. Although they are very thoughtful and giving, they struggle with opening up or expressing their feelings. They need to trust the other person before showing their weakness or vulnerability. Romantic and charming, they will show they care in their own way, like remembering certain details about the person or their birthday. They will be emotionally reserved initially, but only because they like to take things slowly. They will express their love only when they are 100% sure about their feelings.

### Taurus Rising at Home

Think of a Taurus rise like Monica Gellar from Friends. A person can't just move around their furniture. Because they have expensive taste, they usually have high-quality furniture or unique pieces of art. They basically have the best in everything because they enjoy the attention and showing off. However, since they crave stability, they will make sure to choose long-lasting things. They will also focus on their home's lighting as it sets the vibe for the place.

# Quiz

Is your rising sign Aries or Taurus? Take this quiz to find out.

1. Do you make fast decisions?
    - Yes
    - No

2. Would you quit your job to start your own business?
   - Yes
   - No
3. Do you work on more than one project at a time and rarely finish any?
   - Yes
   - No
4. Do your friends often tell you that you need to be more patient?
   - Yes
   - No
5. Do you lead an active and fast-paced life?
   - Yes
   - No
6. If someone asks you to go bungee jumping tomorrow (or on any adventurous experience), will you go?
   - Yes
   - No
7. Do you get frustrated when you have a lot of free time on your hands?
   - Yes
   - No
8. Do you have a hot temper?
   - Yes
   - No
9. Do you say things as they are without sugar-coating your words?
   - Yes
   - No

# Results

If you answered "Yes" to most questions, your rising sign is Aries. If you answered mostly "No," then your rising sign is Taurus.

Taurus and Aries zodiac signs have a few things in common. For instance, their work ethics, loyalty to their partner, stubbornness, appreciation for privacy, and paying attention to their appearance. However, they are different in other aspects. Aries rising individuals are risk-takers and like to do things fast, while Taurus rising individuals are calm and like to work at their own pace.

# Chapter 5: Gemini Rising and Cancer Rising

Following the pattern of the previous chapter, this one breaks down another two similar rising signs - Gemini and Cancer. You'll learn about each sign's personality, how their mind works and how they relate to people around them -whether it comes to professional or personal relationships. And, if you are curious about whether your rising sign is Gemini or Cancer, you'll also be able to find out at the end of the chapter.

## Gemini Rising Sign

### Gemini Rising's Glyph

Gemini symbol.
Bruce The Deus, CC BY-SA 4.0 <https://creativecommons.org/licenses/by-sa/4.0>, via Wikimedia Commons: https://commons.wikimedia.org/wiki/File:Deus_Gemini.png

### Gemini Rising's Personality

Ruled by the planet of communication and intellect, Gemini rising is characterized by an inquisitive and sharp personality. They are known to be open-minded and vivacious, often surrounded by an air of mischief.

They always have something exciting to add to their conversations, whether that is an interesting piece of information they've recently learned or simple gossip. This sign finds everything so fascinating that they can't help but ask questions, especially if they're in a new setting. They notice everything, right down to the last detail make sure they don't miss anything interesting. Since not many people possess this ability, it gives Gemini rising a clear advantage as they'll now have even more information to share. However, keeping up with their conversations can be a grueling task. When excited, Gemini rising will speak fast and jump through topics so quickly that they must be reminded to slow down. They usually respond well to this and will try to listen to others as well. This sign will soak up everything they hear. If you tell them something and forget about it, they will certainly remember it and will be happy to recite it to you.

Due to their adaptable nature, they thrive on variety and are happy to experiment. While they are often criticized for this type of behavior, it helps them see things from a different perspective - which not many people are capable of doing. Together with these traits, the free-flowing personality of the Gemini rising sign also makes them easily influenced by the other signs. Since their individual characteristics will vary depending on other influences on their chart, people born under the Gemini rising signs are the hardest personalities to pin down. And sometimes, it even creates difficulties for Gemini rising themselves when trying to analyze their own behavior.

### Gemini Rising's Mindset

Since communication is so important to this sign, the easiest way to analyze the mindset of Gemini rising is through their social interactions. They use their wit and intellect to win people over. While this may not be a conscious act initially, they will want to keep them around as soon as they come across an interesting person. This is because the more interconnected they are within different communities, the more likely their chances are to explore new horizons. They know that listening is just as key to successful communication as speaking, so they will make a point of being good listeners. Because of this, they can absorb an enormous amount of information they can use to their advantage. They have curious minds and will find a purpose for everything they learn. They are constantly analyzing their environment, which lets them find creative solutions to every problem they encounter. Their inventive mind often drives them to take on projects they don't finish simply because they lose interest and find something more exciting to do.

### Gemini Rising at Work

Gemini rising constantly needs change, which is also reflected in their career choices. They'll opt for professions where they'll have plenty of opportunities to grow and develop new skills. And when they've learned everything they can at their current workplace, they'll move on to another job that lets them expand their mind even further. They also prefer working in an environment where they can communicate with people regularly. They can adapt quickly to any changes in the circumstances and love to find solutions to problems. The more chaotic the atmosphere is, the better. It will stimulate their mind, which works even better under pressure. Gemini rising may want to work with children because they can keep up with kids better than most people. They can also work in any creative field, as their mind is always filled with ideas.

### Gemini Rising in Relationships

Because of their tendency to constantly seek novelties, Gemini rising isn't exactly known as someone who settles into relationships easily. They will constantly seek new acquaintances but may abandon them just as quickly when they lose interest. This is not to say they don't want to establish a committed relationship. It just means they are waiting for the perfect match or someone who challenges them and keeps up with their adventures and fast-paced life. Gemini rising will be a fiercely loyal partner when they find this person, even putting aside their closely guarded interests. They will go out of their way to spend time with their partner and give them everything they need.

### Gemini Rising in Friendships

Gemini risings thrive on social interactions. They'll master the art of navigating multiple conversations and keeping up with everyone around them without even trying. They do put effort into keeping up with the friendships they value. The fact that they have a large social circle doesn't mean they are close to all those people. Despite this, people seem to gravitate towards them and will try to make friends with them. Of course, Gemini rising will be happy to talk to them and form new friendships though they'll choose who they associate with. This sign will be playful when they are with close friends and display incredible wit. They like to inform their friends about everything they've recently learned. Depending on their zodiac placements, Gemini rising may or may not share their opinion through other means. Introverts with this rising sign may feel more comfortable sharing everything they learned through art. Either way, their friends will always feel comfortable talking to them about anything.

### Gemini Rising in Love

Unlike some other rising signs, Gemini is not exactly subtle about their love life. They are typically very blunt about their intentions and will use shocking statements and jokes to pique the interest of a potential partner. They are interested in people who can keep up with their intense communication. They show interest by asking as many questions as possible as if they were conducting a job interview. With a potential romantic partner, Gemini may also put conscious effort into maintaining eye contact - which is not something they usually do as their minds are too busy to focus. They also show affection by touch and offer a sincere friendship, which takes a significant effort on their part.

### Gemini Rising at Home

Thriving in fast-paced environments, Gemini rising isn't exactly the domestic type. They don't feel the need to seek out the comfort of their home life, at least not if they don't have a trustworthy person to share it with. If they establish a stable home life, they want it to be dynamic, bright, and welcoming to the many guests they'll be receiving. However, even in this case, they look at home as a temporary setting, as they will most likely move on to a different one as soon as they hear the call of a new adventure. For them, home is more about who they surround themselves with and not a place to spend time in.

# Cancer Rising Sign

## Cancer Rising's Glyph

Cancer symbol.
Bruce The Deus, CC BY-SA 4.0 <https://creativecommons.org/licenses/by-sa/4.0>, via Wikimedia Commons: https://commons.wikimedia.org/wiki/File:Deus_Cancer.png

### Cancer Rising's Personality

The core personality of a Cancer rising is built on values like resilience and being attuned to people around them. They constantly interact with the world and care about how they are viewed. This sign isn't afraid to launch into new ventures, driven by their emotions or by someone else. While some would consider being so emotional a weakness, Cancer rising learns how to make the most of it by turning it into their greatest strength. Their shining personalities are a balm to others, but they can absorb other people's energies. If this other person has a sensitive personality, the loyal Cancer rising will display the same traits. These displays of loyalty often only last until the person leaves the room. As soon as a different type of energy surrounds the Cancer, their personality will change to match it. Their personality is also affected by the moon's cycles - which probably explains why their moods shift so often. One minute they feel peachy and act with empathy, and the next, they will close off and retreat into their figurative shells. And just as the moon goes through different cycles, so will a Cancer rising sign. This allows them to experience a multifaceted life many people only dream of having.

Not only do Cancer rising have highly intuitive personalities, but they don't hide it either. They won't shy away from expressing their opinion or sharing their emotions and personal information. They are happy to embrace different circumstances and will tell you what they think. And if they don't, their mood will signal whatever type of energy they are currently affected by. At the same time, they also like to control everything around them - including what they show to others of themselves. It doesn't always work, but they are much happier if they can share only positive thoughts and emotions. More likely than not, at your first meeting, you'll get the feeling that they are easy-going people with a friendly attitude when, in fact, they are probably just as nervous as the next person. They will certainly worry about what impression they'll make on you, even if you can't tell this at the beginning.

### Cancer Rising's Mindset

Many of the Cancer risings' thought processes are ruled by their emotions. On the one hand, this sign values their emotions and will often tap into them when they are trying to make a decision. On the other hand, Cancer rising is also sensitive to other people's feelings, and being tuned into these emotional stimuli often overwhelms their thoughts. Despite this, their philosophy is to help out whenever they can, even if it costs them their stability. After all, they can always regroup and continue with their life later on. They also consider that the level of loyalty they give has to be earned. They would rather be cautious at the beginning, so they can let their guard down later, than go all in at first and be surprised by their mistake. Another trait of their mindset is that they love order in all aspects of their lives. If something is out of order, they will do everything they can to remedy the situation. Not only that, but they will offer to do this for others as well.

### Cancer Rising at Work

People with a Cancer rising sign are natural-born leaders and love working in a fast-paced setting. They will constantly work toward new goals, and if they have to compete against others to reach them, even better. They are not ruthless or unfeeling toward their competition. They simply love to feel like they are moving forward with their professional lives. Since they thrive on a structured schedule, Cancer rising will choose self-employment.

They'll even consider careers that many consider too risky, such as creative arts or running their own freelance businesses. If they believe they can do it, they will follow through, no matter what anyone else says. Depending on their zodiac placements, Cancer rising may prefer a career that keeps them on the move, or they may want to work with people. Their compassionate and tender nature makes them perfect for becoming a therapist.

### Cancer Rising in Relationships

Starting a relationship with a Cancer rising isn't the easiest thing to do. They will be interested and even act friendly, but some of their cordiality will be superficial. And while they don't particularly worry that someone will hurt them, they are very picky about how they share their emotions. They will need to test their partner and get to know them before they are ready to form deeper emotional bonds. Partners shouldn't be surprised if they can't get much out of them on the personal front, either. Cancer rising is very aware of the importance of surrounding themselves with people who positively impact their life. The person they form a relationship with is someone who affects their life's course, so it's understandably crucial for them to be able to trust that person. In well-established relationships, Cancer rising is a partner who always motivates and challenges their partners to take on new adventures. They can only be happy with someone who shares their love for being in motion and helping others.

### Cancer Rising in Friendships

Cancer rising is a very wise and dependable sign. Most of the time, they are the friend that cheers you up with a joke or two when you are feeling down or simply lets you vent about the stressful day you had at your job. However, this can be draining for their own emotional state, and Cancer rising isn't afraid to admit this. They will state that they need some time alone and expect everyone to respect their emotions just as they've respected anyone else. That's not to say they won't feel guilty for not being there for their friends 24/7. However, to avoid feeling overstimulated, they must take time off. Once they are recharged, they will return to looking out for their friends and showing their loyalty whenever needed. In fact, they are so good at matching their friends' energies that someone outside their social circle will never be able to tell whether a Cancer rising is expressing their opinion or just being loyal to their friends.

### Cancer Rising in Love

Cancer rising is always looking for the mysterious and all-consuming love - but when they find it, they are careful how to approach this situation. They are protective of their feelings and rarely express them to their partner, which complicates their love life. They will show affection through other means, such as seeking physical proximity, asking about the partner's interests, and making silly jokes. Rather than telling someone that they are interested in them, they will drop little hints. However, expecting the other person to pick up their signal often backfires as their messages tend to be far less obvious than they think they are.

### Cancer Rising at Home

Because of their nurturing nature, Cancer rising considers home life extremely important. They like to come home after their latest adventure and rest for a bit before moving on to the next one. Because of this, they want their home to be inviting and will take great care of it and who they invite into it. At the same time, they like things to be organized, as it helps them run everything smoothly.

# Quiz

Is your rising sign Gemini or Cancer? Take this quiz to find out.

1. Do you often take on a broad point of view rather than a deep one?
   - Yes
   - No
2. Would you quit your job to travel around the world?
   - Yes
   - No
3. Do you constantly need to do something, even if it's only talking to someone?
   - Yes
   - No

4. Do you get bored easily in familiar settings?
   - Yes
   - No
5. Do you have an active and multifaceted social life?
   - Yes
   - No
6. Are you quick to adapt to changes in your life?
   - Yes
   - No
7. Is being an intelligent person with unique interests the first impression you leave?
   - Yes
   - No
8. Are you insecure about your skills and abilities?
   - Yes
   - No
9. Have you ever been told that you ask too many questions?
   - Yes
   - No

## Results

If you answered "Yes" to most questions, your rising sign is Gemini. If you answered mostly "No," then your rising sign is Cancer.

Gemini has an active mind and a tendency to communicate and soak in knowledge any way it comes. They are social butterflies ready to embrace variety and will even seek it out. The reason lies in their own dual personality - Gemini is open-minded about other people's feelings and opinions, yet so insecure about their own. While Cancer rising is similarly affectionate and generous with their feelings, they require more stability. They also place more importance on past events and will seek refuge in familiar places from time to time.

# Chapter 6: Leo Rising and Virgo Rising

Now that we've looked at the rising signs for Aries, Taurus, Gemini, and Cancer, we'll look at the Leo and Virgo rising signs. As in previous chapters, we look at the personalities and mindsets of individuals with these signs, as well as how they act at work, in relationships and friendships, at home, and when they are in love.

## Leo Rising Sign

Leo Rising's Glyph

Leo symbol.
*Bruce The Deus, CC BY-SA 4.0 <https://creativecommons.org/licenses/by-sa/4.0>, via Wikimedia Commons: https://commons.wikimedia.org/wiki/File:Deus_Leo.png*

The word "Leo" means "lion." In Greek mythology, the constellation was associated with the legendary Nemean Lion. This glyph is a stylized representation of a lion's head and tail or its mane and spine.

Some versions of this glyph include curved shapes inside the circle. These shapes are interpreted as stylized representations of the two halves of a heart.

### Leo Rising's Personality

Leo is a fire sign; people born under it burn as brightly as the sun. They are bright and friendly and are the life and soul of the party as soon as they step into a room. They are confident, optimistic, warm, and always ready to take a stand for things they truly believe in.

This attitude toward life earns them a lot of friends, and they're rarely seen alone. These individuals like to stand out and, like the sun, are bright and flashy, so you won't miss them when you see them in a group.

At the same time, they have a good helping of self-regard. While self-confidence isn't bad, people born under Leo Rising can occasionally take things to the next level and become arrogant and egotistic. This can have a negative impact on their personal relationships.

People born under Leo rising love to show off. This isn't limited to boasting about their own achievements – they also take pride in their loved ones, particularly their children. At the same time, they can be controlling. They consider their creations as extensions of themselves, including their spouses and children.

Because of this, these individuals will find it difficult to collaborate with or work under people with stronger personalities than their own.

At the same time, people with this rising sign have a natural tendency for leadership. As natural-born leaders, their charisma makes them even more attractive to the people they lead. They love nothing better than being visibly appreciated and cheered on, and a leadership position gives them exactly this opportunity.

These individuals have a powerful desire to feel important and gain the approval of others. If they feel they are receiving the appreciation that they deserve, they return to their fun, life-of-the-party personality. However, if they feel not enough people are noticing them, they can get stuck sulking until they get the attention they need.

Leo rising individuals also tend to have larger-than-life aspirations and attitudes. They are all about grand gestures, and they believe that, more than anything else, life is meant to be enjoyed to the fullest. These individuals live life royally, as implied by the symbol (lion) of their rising sign.

If the pride of these individuals is injured, their temper will flare easily. However, though Leo risings are quick-tempered, they're also inherently easy-going, which means their anger rarely lasts for long.

Leo risings are faithful to a fault and will never cheat or harm the people they consider their own. At the same time, their lives are bound to be dramatic, so the people close to them should expect that the Leo rising in their life will constantly demand attention, playing and discarding many roles until they find one that suits them.

No matter what traits the Leo rising in your life shows as prominent, one thing is for certain: living with these individuals is certainly never boring!

### Leo Rising's Mindset

The Leo rising mindset can be best described as one of clear and strong intentions. These individuals take pride in clearly understanding where they want to go, and no matter where this journey takes them, they will not falter until they achieve what they want. In some ways, they can be described as having a one-track mind, though this isn't necessarily a fair description; it's closer to the truth to say that once they have decided on a goal, there's very little in the world that can sway them away from it.

This is because Leo Risings do not tolerate failure. They value having the comfort of a plan and don't do well when forced to deviate from it. Luckily, they also know the value of surrounding themselves with high-achieving people, so they're rarely unsuccessful.

### Leo Rising at Work

As mentioned, Leo risings values have a plan to fall back upon. They won't be spontaneous and unexpected in their decisions, but this doesn't mean they don't take risks – it simply means they aren't fans of "winging" things. If they're forced to work without having a plan, they'll become stressed and irritated.

They value hard work and will always conduct themselves professionally – but, at the same time, their charm means their every action seems calm and leisurely. Don't be fooled by the façade, however – there's a reason Leo risings shine so brightly, and it's *not because of a carefree attitude to life and work.*

### Leo Rising in Relationships

In relationships, these individuals are always willing to lend an empathetic ear and shoulder, especially if you're very close to them. However, they are natural charmers, so people often mistake their natural friendliness for actual friendship.

While Leo risings are friendly with most people around them, true friendship is reserved for a select few. This isn't to say they'll be rude or unpleasant to people; it simply means, in their mind, the distinction between friend and acquaintance is clear, and it's always best to know where you stand if only to prevent heartache for yourself.

### Leo Rising in Friendships

If you're friends with a Leo rising, you have a true friend for life. These individuals give everything they have to the people they care about and are the most loyal friends you'll ever have.

From spending hours looking for a solution to your problems to being available for your important occasions, a Leo rising will do it all for the people in their close circle. Their hearts are as big as the sun, and when they share theirs with you, you'll know you have a friend for a lifetime.

Don't step on their friendship, however. These individuals are guarded because they have been burned before; if you take advantage of them, they will neither forget nor forgive.

**Leo Rising in Love**

Just as they are loyal to their friends and family, Leo risings are also loyal to their partners. They will never cheat on you, and with a Leo rising as a partner, you never have to worry about being betrayed.

These individuals are natural givers and will ensure you have everything you want and need. They love to care for their partners, and their way of showing their love includes cheerleading their partner, acts of service, and words of affirmation.

They love to show off the people they care for, and if you're in a relationship with a Leo, that will mean you, so be ready for their attention to be all yours! Leo risings will always show up for you, make you feel valued, and are great partners.

**Leo Rising at Home**

Leo risings know the value of appearances, which extends to their home. While they may not come from wealth, they appreciate life's finer things and will look for hours to find the perfect items to decorate their homes. Other people may think that a Leo rising's home is a bit too ostentatious for them, but it's undeniable that everything is of high quality.

At the same time, these individuals love their privacy. They do not easily let other people into their sanctuary and safe space, so if you're invited to their home, treat it as a gift for what it is. When you visit, make sure you complement their home as it's a surefire way to make them feel appreciated and score a return invitation.

# Virgo Rising Sign

## Virgo Rising's Glyph

Virgo symbol.
Bruce The Deus, CC BY-SA 4.0 <https://creativecommons.org/licenses/by-sa/4.0>, via Wikimedia Commons: https://commons.wikimedia.org/wiki/File:Deus_Virgo.png

The word "Virgo" means "maiden," and, in Greek mythology, the constellation was associated with various goddesses – generally either goddesses related to wheat (such as Demeter and Persephone) or virgin/maiden goddesses (such as Astraea).

This glyph comes from the Greek letters ΠΑΡ. These letters are an abbreviation of the word "*parthenos*," the Greek word for "virgin." Another interpretation of this glyph is that it represents a maiden carrying a shaft of wheat.

## Virgo Rising's Personality

The Virgo rising individual is conscientious, well put-together, and organized. They are reliable and can be perfectionists, but they also have enormously trustworthy personalities. They are purposeful and can be obsessed with cleanliness and tidying up.

These people are logical and pragmatic and can be bluntly honest in their analysis of other people. This can make them come across as cold and aloof, but it's a quality they also use on themselves.

They are ambitious and self-motivated, so, unlike many other rising signs, they're not dependent on outside encouragement. They are humble, self-effacing at times, and have a drive towards being of service. They have a need to be productive, and their big heart means this will be shown by helping the people around them.

They are always looking for ways to improve themselves. They often struggle with insecurity, though their desire to fix things occasionally makes them seem negative and critical of the people around them. However, this couldn't be further from the truth. Rather, their struggle with insecurity means their criticism is usually directed inward at their own selves.

They enjoy patterns and balance around them and can be extremely disconcerted when faced with change, especially major change. Their need for balance also means they tend to worry a lot and become very anxious when faced with new and unexpected situations.

They are kind and good-tempered but, at the same time, enjoy their privacy. Their logical side will find it challenging to express themselves, especially if they haven't had time to mull over every possible outcome of their words.

At the extreme, they can become obsessive perfectionists, which often causes people to mistake them as being dull and boring.

Mercury rules a Virgo rising, the planet of communication, and, as a result, they are quick-thinking and curious about the world around them. However, the planet Chiron (a minor planet in astronomy) also influences Virgos, which is where their logical and guarded nature comes from.

These individuals are also considered to be the healers of the zodiac. While they're unlikely to let many people see the real them, their caring nature, call to service, and altruism means they are always willing to help people around them. They are loyal and supportive and will always be considerate of your emotions.

However, they are susceptible to falling prey to their more judgmental tendencies in extreme cases. They are not only critical of others. They are extremely critical of themselves as well. If they aren't able to complete tasks they have set for themselves to the standards they expect, they are very hard on themselves, to the point where their mental health could suffer.

Others can find their observant, perfectionist natures intimidating. However, once you get to know the Virgo rising, you'll soon realize that they're anything but intimidating, and your life will be all the richer for it.

### Virgo Rising's Mindset

Though Virgo risings are fond of change, they're also well aware that the world is constantly changing around them. In some ways, this is what makes them so resistant to change. They are desperate to maintain the ground on which they have built their world, which can make them appear guarded.

However, this desire to prevent change does have a silver lining. Virgo risings know that relationships of all kinds need to be maintained, and they are always willing to put in that effort. At the same time, they crave peace and security, which means they always approach life with a plan. This can mean something as innocuous as stocking up on products for their home in advance of their needs, or on the other end of the scale, can make them hesitant to take action without considering every possibility, which often results in them missing out on important opportunities.

### Virgo Rising at Work

Virgo risings are ambitious and self-motivated. They work tirelessly toward being successful at work, and their love of service means they are always willing to dedicate hours to things they consider to be worthy causes. If they can see the goal they've been aiming for in the mirror or the light at the end of the tunnel they want to reach, they're completely capable of speeding things up so they can reach their final destination without compromising the quality of their work.

While they might seem unapproachable, they thrive when working in a community of like-minded people. While they are working alone, being connected to people around them gives them additional incentive to keep going. So, if you work with a Virgo rising individual, make sure you get in touch with them often, as you'll find no better coworkers when you're working towards a common goal.

### Virgo Rising in Relationships

If you can get past the intimidating hard shell often put out by a Virgo rising, you'll quickly find that they are pleasant and kind individuals. It may take them time to figure out the best way to connect with you, but they won't look back once they do. When they're close to a person, they are compassionate and understanding. All they ask is that you be there to match their energy and grow with them side-by-side.

### Virgo Rising in Friendships

Virgo risings are dedicated friends and are often the first port of call when their loved ones are hurt. Though they can be hard to get to know, once they feel comfortable with you, they will always be there to help, no matter when you need them.

However, they can also be very private with their own emotions and often exclude close friends and partners from what is going on in their minds. This can sometimes cause issues in friendships, as some people will believe that a Virgo rising's inability to share parts of themselves unbalances their relationship. However, if you can be patient with these individuals and work with their need for logic and certainty, you'll soon find them opening up to you.

While their logical thinking can make it seem like they're unable to be affectionate toward their friends, they'll be loyal and present when you need them to be.

### Virgo Rising in Love

Virgo risings are devoted partners. They enjoy being in love, even if they can seem a bit closed off and hard to get to know.

As the partner to a Virgo rising, it's essential to understand how they communicate nonverbally. Getting them to open up as much as you would like in a romantic relationship can often be challenging, but once you're in tune with what they're saying nonverbally, you'll quickly realize that they're quite expressive.

Keep in mind that, while they won't vocalize them, Virgo risings feel emotions deeply. This is especially true in romantic relationships, and they're unlikely to enter into a romance without having long-term expectations. So, if you're not serious about a relationship, don't step into one with a Virgo rising.

### Virgo Rising at Home

Virgo risings are extremely curious and always looking for ways to bring the world into their homes. Even if they have not had the opportunity to travel extensively, they are always looking for ways to understand other perspectives, and their home décor and the contents of their bookshelves often reflect this.

They're always prepared for everything, which is reflected in their home. They want to have resources on hand, whether it is a well-stocked first aid kit or a comprehensive guide to topics they are interested in. At the same time, their home is their fortress and a way for them to reach their inner Zen, so if you're looking for a housewarming present for these individuals, a book on their current topic of interest or a therapeutic candle will not be unappreciated.

Now that we've looked at six of the 12 rising signs, the next step is to look at the other signs. Turn the page to learn more about the Libra and Scorpio rising signs. After that, we'll cover Sagittarius and Capricorn rising and Aquarius and Pisces rising.

# Chapter 7: Libra Rising and Scorpio Rising

This chapter will focus on the Libra and Scorpio rising signs and discuss their personality traits and mindsets. Like in the previous chapters, you will get to understand how each of these signs deals with various parts of their lives, including work, relationships, friendships, love, and their homes.

## Libra Rising Sign

### Libra Rising's Glyph

Libra symbol.
Bruce The Deus, CC BY-SA 4.0 <https://creativecommons.org/licenses/by-sa/4.0>, via Wikimedia Commons: https://commons.wikimedia.org/wiki/File:Deus_Libra.png

### Libra Rising's Personality

A Libra rising is the person to go to if you ever need a peacemaker. These individuals are excellent at maintaining peace and tranquility. They will do anything, even if it means they need to compromise, or even give up their own comfort if it means that everyone else will be happy. Their caring nature, even when dealing with strangers, is what makes them lovable and popular. They are great to be around.

Being the charming individuals they are, it should come as no surprise that Venus rules Libra risings. It is known for being the planet of love, passion, and everything beautiful. The older they get, the better they can master their captivating aura. They are naturally flirtatious and seductive. They know how to get in touch with their senses. When they are balanced and doing well, people find Libra risings very addictive. Influenced by Venus, these individuals are highly intoxicating. It can be very hard to stay away from them.

Libra is a cardinal sign, one of three astrological modalities or qualities. Cardinal signs are associated with the seasons since they start the seasonal cycles. Libra, the air sign, is associated with autumn. This means that Libra marks the start of the fall equinox. Cardinal signs are known for initiating change and their leadership skills. They like planning, visualizing, goal setting, and doing everything that brings them closer to their dreams. They are blessed with emotional and social intelligence, determination, and the important quality of self-initiation. But cardinal signs are susceptible to pessimism and absorbing negativity from others.

Libras are always on the go. They like to ensure that their voices are heard and their opinions are valued. The best thing about Libra risings is that they make their presence known with charm are grace. Libras are not loud. They don't seek attention, but instead, they earn it. This quality is very useful in a leadership role. The sign of Libra is represented by a scale, which shows how orderly this sign is. They like things to be symmetrical and seek balance in all areas of life.

Libra rising individuals are talkative and friendly. They have no problem walking up to anyone and conversing with them about anything and everything. If you struggle with social anxiety or often worry about awkward silence, a Libra rising can be the friend you never knew you needed. Libra risings are approachable and extroverted while maintaining respect and courtesy. They are very polite and are highly aware of those around them. They try to relate to others in all situations, encouraging people to warm up to them easily.

Libra risings are very intelligent. This is due to their open-mindedness and their ability to find compromises. They are problem-solvers and creative thinkers. They are also gentle and soft and approach all their interactions and tasks with care. Their delicacy shows in how they behave, move, think, and speak.

These individuals are also known for their kind-heartedness. Even though the inclination toward leadership sometimes makes them bossy, Libra rising individuals are generally sweet. They avoid conflicts and chaos whenever possible because balance and harmony are their priority. This is why they're very picky when it comes to who they choose to surround themselves with. They know better than to get involved in drama.

Even though they're very picky about those who make it into their circle, Libra risings are fun to be around. They are calm and joyful without even trying. It's best, however, if you always stay on their good side.

**Libra Rising's Mindset**

As mentioned above, Libra rising individuals are self-motivated; they don't need outside pressure to accomplish a task. A Libra rising's life mission is to experience endless happiness and good vibes. They want to maintain positive vibes and go with the flow of things. They don't like to over-complicate situations because they don't allow fear to hold them back.

Libra risings don't like staying in one place for too long. They are either up for changes or working on self-growth and development. If your ascendant is Libra, you probably don't dwell on unfortunate turns of events. You know that the world will go on, whether you like it or not. This doesn't mean you're emotionless, detached, or don't care. In fact, Libra risings are very in touch with their emotions. They just don't want to be stuck in them.

### Libra Rising at Work

At work, you'll find Libra risings are the mediators of the team. They make compromises and find the middle ground in all interactions. This makes them great negotiators. This makes them great lawyers, judges, government officials, and diplomats in general. Libra risings are extremely ambitious and will go above and beyond to make its ideas happen. They're also very secretive regarding work, so they don't share the details with anyone. They know what they need to do, so they move in silence.

Their ambition and vast imagination allow them to succeed in creative fields. They also make good consultants. Since Libras are always on the move, sitting them down at a desk or giving them a strict timeline to stick to can be quite stressful and overwhelming. They thrive in work environments where they can enjoy a sense of freedom that enables them to work at their own pace. While this isn't necessarily bad, it can put them at risk of procrastination. Once they put their mind to it, they'll dive right into the task at hand. Libra rising like volunteer work, community building, and networking. They are often concerned with social causes and take on major activist roles.

### Libra Rising in Relationships

Libra risings are very independent. They enjoy having people that they can trust and rely on in life. They like loving relationships and motivating connections that promote personal growth. Libra risings are lovers, not fighters. That said, they will only settle for people who are as self-motivated as the average Libra is. They appreciate emotions and the expression of love. However, they can't stand clinginess. They have strong boundaries in place.

Libra risings feel their best when like-minded individuals surround them. They love building relationships with optimistic, industrious, and inspiring people. They don't have any time to waste, so they won't give any chances to people who vibrate on lower frequencies.

### Libra Rising in Friendships

Libra risings are very friendly and respectful. They may get a little flirty too. However, be careful not to take it too personally or feel flattered by their charm. They will go to great lengths to satiate the needs of the people they love. Libra risings are compatible with other rising air signs: Aquarius and Gemini. They are also compatible with fire signs Leo, Aries, and Sagittarius. Libra risings are least compatible with water signs, especially Scorpio rising and Pisces rising.

### Libra Rising in Love

Libra rising individuals are natural-born activists. They are concerned with the greater good of the community, meaning that they will appreciate their partner being aware of the issues that impact the world. This is because Libra risings view love as an opportunity to share their passions, interests, and hobbies with the person they love. They will sit down and watch the football game with you if that's what you like to do.

### Libra Rising at Home

Libra risings value order and structure. They are disciplined individuals who perform best when their home is clean and clutter-free. Their lives can get very busy, so having a home where they can relax is very important. Libra risings are known for their expensive taste. It can also take them a while to arrange their space exactly how they like it.

## Scorpio Rising Sign

### Scorpio Rising's Glyph

Scorpio symbol.
Bruce The Deus, CC BY-SA 4.0 <https://creativecommons.org/licenses/by-sa/4.0>, via Wikimedia Commons: https://commons.wikimedia.org/wiki/File:Deus_Scorpio.png

### Scorpio Rising's Personality

Having the water sign, Scorpio, as your ascendant can make you appear quite mysterious. Everything about you, from your behavior to your appearance, can lead people to perceive you as a bit standoffish or unapproachable, at least when they first meet you. This is because Scorpios are very guarded and find it hard to open up to new people. They can't shake the fact that the world can sometimes be a dangerous place to live in, which is why they seldom let anyone into theirs.

Scorpio, like Aries, is ruled by Mars. One may think that this planet influences Scorpio the same way that it influences the fire sign, Aries. However, this isn't always the case. While a fiery temperament and rage do emerge at times, imagine a volcano, and you get the idea of the power of the energy exchange. Mars encourages Scorpio rising individuals to bottle up their feelings like lava. Unprocessed emotions sit seething in a sea of torment and self-criticism. Scorpio rising individuals continue to push their feelings down and torment themselves for their shortcomings until they erupt.

Scorpio's astrological modality or trait is fixed. The earth signs Taurus, the fire sign Leo, and the air sign Aquarius are also fixed signs. Each of them is associated with a certain season. Like Libra, Scorpio is associated with the fall.

Unlike the change initiator, Libra, Scorpio, and other fixed signs are natural traditionalists. They are believed to stabilize the zodiac. When we say that Scorpio rising individuals are traditionalists, we don't mean that they are boring or extremely uptight. Tradition here doesn't refer to a fixed routine or the rejection of modern tools and methods. It simply means that they value the meaning behind the actions they take and the things they do.

Scorpions, Taurus's, Leos, and Aquarians are known for their productive, loyal, and creative tendencies. They are also thought to be perfectionists. Fixed signs can get very stubborn. However, the exact manifestation of this trait varies depending on the astrological elements and dynamics of each sign. For instance, Taurus's are stubborn in maintaining structure in their lives. A Leo's stubbornness shows itself when they express the need to be the center of attention. Scorpions often let their emotions influence their ambitions, and Aquarians are stubborn when taking on leadership roles even though they enjoy their freedom.

Once they've set out on a decision or made up their minds about something, it can be impossible to get them to change their minds about it. They will never admit to being wrong or give up on their decision. While this gives them a sense of stability and consistency in their lives, it may also cause them to miss opportunities. Their stubbornness can keep them stuck in one place for too long. It may also cause them to walk down a path they now realize is wrong, just so they don't go back on their word.

Scorpio rising individuals are great at solving problems. They also have a strong eye for detail. They excel in areas that require critical thinking and deep focus. Sometimes, individuals with Scorpio ascending placement can feel out of place. They may feel disconnected from their environment. Their high intuition also causes them to appear somewhat robot-like. Engagement and communicating may not be their strong suit as they are not easy talkers. However, all their actions are highly calculated. They like to roam around the world purposefully and wisely. Going with the flow doesn't always work for them, meaning they always know their next move.

The best thing about a Scorpio rising individual is that they like to fight for the things they believe in. They are characterized by strong will and determination. Scorpio ascendants are known for their charm and allure, mostly from the air of mystery surrounding them. This sense of enigma makes them interesting and attractive to everyone around them. They hold some sort of power that attracts the attention of others. These individuals often seem unapproachable, yet the type of person that many wish to connect with.

People who are reluctant to approach a Scorpio rising individual end up being surprised by their charming personality; expecting a cold or aloof individual, people are often taken aback to find Scorpio risings to be delightful company. People with Scorpio ascendants master this charming aspect of their being because they wish to avoid numerous stupid questions. You will never entirely get to know them unless they let their guard down around you.

The delightful side to a Scorpio rising is not a mere facade. You may be surprised to learn that they are among the most generous and kind-hearted individuals out there. Their detachment and coldness is a protective mechanism.

Perfectionism and ambition run through a Scorpio rising's blood. They don't sit around after completing a task, nor do they take the time to admire or even rethink their work. They are ready to drive into another project right away. Scorpio risings are always on the lookout for great things to accomplish.

### Scorpio Rising's Mindset

Scorpio rising individuals usually feel that no one understands what they're thinking or how they feel. They realize that they are quite complicated, and often, they struggle to understand the world around them too. They are passionate and strong-willed. However, the tiniest shift in their inner or outer balance can cause them to feel a little shaken and even disoriented. This is why they think a lot before they act. Because Scorpio risings spend most of their time being cautious and on edge, they deeply appreciate anyone with whom they can be themselves. They are risk-takers (calculated, of course!). They don't mind venturing – only if they think the experience, cause, or outcome is worth the risk.

### Scorpio Rising at Work

The world of work feels like constant change, new ideas, and endless innovation. This is especially true for the demands placed on employees to be more creative, collaborative, and innovative. In this environment, what does it mean to be a Scorpio working in the world of work? As a sign associated with hidden depths and secretive nature, people who are born under the Scorpio rising are often seen as mysterious and aloof. Despite this common perception of them as loners or hermits, people born under the Scorpio zodiac sign are also known for their strength and courage – traits that will serve them well as they navigate their professional roles. The qualities of being a Scorpio professional are intense focus and dedication coupled with a deep-rooted intensity that can serve as both an asset or liability, depending on the situation.

Their diligence, critical thinking and problem-solving skills, and strong focus make them suitable for disciplines like law, writing, research, and finance. They will take on any challenge that comes their way, which allows them to thrive at work. The best thing about Scorpio risings at work is that their passion never fails to shine. Since they don't have a problem with taking risks, they stand out among their peers in the workplace. They also get things done quickly so they can hop onto the next tasks, making them an asset to the workplace.

### Scorpio Rising in Relationships

These individuals like straightforward relationships. They like easy-going and manageable connections and will avoid dramatic people whenever possible. They value people that they instantly click. They are very intelligent when it comes to capturing subtle hints, clues, and overtones. However, interpreting hidden meanings is not something they want to do throughout the entire relationship. If they constantly must figure out what another person's gestures or words mean, they will quickly lose interest. Communication is not a Scorpio rising's best suit during periods of stress.

### Scorpio Rising in Friendships

Their strong will and inclination to fight for everything that they stand for makes Scorpio risings incompatible with other individuals with Scorpio ascending signs. However, they are still compatible with the water signs Cancer and Pisces. Since they are equally sensual, Scorpio risings tend to be drawn by Taurus risings. They also get along well with Earth signs like Capricorn and Virgo.

Once a Scorpio ascendant reveals their authentic self to you, you will realize that they're the best friend that you've ever had. These individuals go to great lengths to protect the people they care for. They are very loyal and are ready to take your side even when you aren't on the same page. They will explain their point of view but will still defend you until their last breath. They greatly respect people who express their beliefs and speak their minds.

### Scorpio Rising in Love

When it comes to love, Scorpio ascendants may unintentionally send mixed signals. Because of their aloof guise, which they use to protect themselves, they may appear to be head over heels one second and very distant the next. They fear appearing too clingy. However, once they've opened up to you, they can be. They like relationships with long-term potential. They have no interest in superficial connections. These protective individuals will always make you feel loved and safe. Scorpio rising is an intense and passionate sign. They're also secretive and guarded. But once they open up to someone, they have the potential to be one of the strongest and most loyal partners you will ever meet. The best partner for a Scorpio is someone who matches their drive and determination in life — not necessarily anyone with whom they fall in love at first sight. Knowing how to attract a Scorpio in love is important if you want to win their heart. Scorpios love deeply but cautiously. They are passionate about what matters most to them but distrust those who appear too eager to impress them from the get-go.

**Scorpio Rising at Home**

For a Scorpio Rising, their home is their safe haven. It's a den that they can use to escape the hustle and bustle of the real world. This is why they like to ensure that it has everything they could possibly need. They may decorate their home with house plants and paintings to give it a more relaxing feel. Scorpio risings are either into smart homes and futuristic designs or have very minimalistic tastes. Regarding the home, there are few other signs like Scorpio; they love the finer things in life and won't hesitate to spend their money on luxurious items that have special meaning to them. In addition, as we discussed previously, Scorpios spend a great deal of time in their homes. They are quite private individuals, so living in large homes might not be ideal for this sign.

# Chapter 8: Sagittarius Rising and Capricorn Rising

This chapter expands on Sagittarius rising and Capricorn rising signs. It explains how the rising signs affect your life. People who were born during these periods display traits that make them different from other individuals. Sagittarius and Capricorn are two very different rising signs with very different outlooks on life. While Sagittarius is open, optimistic, and adventurous, Capricorn is reserved, cautious and realistic. As a result, when these two signs come together in the same person, the result is an interesting mixture of both signs' positive and negative traits. Depending on whether you have Capricorn or Sagittarius rising, this can have several implications for your character. Let's take a closer look.

# Sagittarius Rising

Sagittarius symbol.
Bruce The Deus, CC BY-SA 4.0 <https://creativecommons.org/licenses/by-sa/4.0>, via Wikimedia Commons: https://commons.wikimedia.org/wiki/File:Deus_Sagittarius.png

People born when the Sun's horizon was in the same range as the sign of Sagittarius are usually found somewhere on a trip. To meet the Sagittarius rising, you need to travel since these people love traveling to learn history and are explorers at heart. They always try to move out of their comfort zone.

Sagittarius rising people are always interested in learning new things to expand their knowledge. They are optimistic and believe they can achieve great things that are often viewed as impossible. Their personalities are charming, and people are ready to help them realize their goals. They are also jokesters who make other people happy. Sagittarius Risings consists of people who love the truth. Although they may not realize it, they will use different means to attain the information they want. They don't want to live in the dark.

## The Sagittarius Rising Mindset

Let's face it: We all have those days when it feels like the world is against us. Even though Sagittarius rising is known for its optimistic nature, even they can fall victim to occasional bouts of pessimism and self-doubt. But, as with all of us, what matters most is how we respond to these situations. Will we let them bring us down, or will we rise above them? The latter is what being a Sagittarius is all about. Let's take a look at why this sign is so optimistic and how we can stay that way on even the darkest of days.

Sagittarius risings focus mainly on growth, optimism, and positivity. The Sagittarius rising mindset reflects a risk-taking personality. They appreciate the things that belong to them but can go the extra mile to expand their knowledge by seeking answers to what they may not understand. Sagittarius energy is concerned with adventures and awareness that make them feel extraordinary. What they do not want is to feel misinformed or to ever appear mediocre.

### Sagittarius Rising at Work

Sagittarius Risings can be a bit stubborn and are often over-ambitious. Most of them are talkative because Jupiter, their ruler, is primarily concerned with growth. As a result, the Sagittarius risings are interested in developing multiple talents and skills. Ironically, the Sagittarius risings are slow movers, although they are flexible when it comes to gaining new knowledge. Their method of work, while sometimes believed to be slow, is not a setback since they take pride in everything they do.

They are life learners and see each task as a wonderful opportunity to learn something new. The Sagittarius risings love to research and reflect on how the knowledge they acquire impact their life. These people are perfectionists and want to ensure In the workplace, they are focused and insightful. However, their biggest challenge is that they can be stubborn and judgmental, which may not go down well with co-workers.

### Sagittarius Risings in Relationships

Sagittarius Risings find relationships easy since they have charming personalities. They are magnetic and attract many people. They can appeal to like-minded people who help them shape their opinions and ideas. The Sagittarius risings are careful when it comes to engaging with other people. They want to deal with smart people with whom they can meaningfully interact. They can also freely share their ideas when the right people surround them.

When the Sagittarius risings are with their close friends, they are conversational and open to different opinions. Many people admire their way of dealing with different situations. However, they can be a little blunt in some instances.

### Sagittarius Rising and Love

In terms of love affairs, Sagittarius risings are practical. They are realistic and interested in dealing with reality to choose the appropriate people they can associate with. + They can be picky about the person they choose as a partner. These individuals can also fight for the people they are strongly attached to. When they look for a partner, they know what they are interested in, making them free to display an open mind.

Sagittarius risings like experimenting with different things and exploring new environments to improve their knowledge. At worst, these individuals can rush into love and often find themselves out within a short time. Many people struggle with tempo when it comes to relationships.

### Home and Sagittarius Rising

With their natural thirst for adventure and love of travel, Sagittarian risings can thrive away from home. But they need to be in a home environment where they can thrive. The good news is that there are many ways you can feel at peace at home. You can do small things that will have a big impact on your life and happiness.

Sagittarius risings often feel at peace when they are at home. They do not consider every place they visit home because it may lack the facilities that give them total comfort. They feel at home if they find a comfortable space where they can perform their favorite hobbies. It can also be a local pub where they can enjoy their favorite drink and play a pool game. In other words, a home is a place that brings peace and tranquility.

### Time of Excess

A Sagittarius rising's faith dwindles at some point, and they become despondent if they fail to find the answers they are looking for. Sagittarius risings are usually optimistic, but they need to be careful and avoid situations where they can set unrealistic goals that are difficult to achieve, which leads to disappointment. They also tend to overstep the mark or inflate their ego, but this does not always produce the desired results. This can lead to undesired behavior if you fail to achieve your goals.

The bad thing about over-optimism is that it can lead to recklessness, greed, or lack of due caution. If they go to extremes, they could end up believing they are invincible, which is not true, and the crash will be very hurtful when they realize the truth.

### Truth Sharing

If Sagittarius is your Ascendant, you must explore different things that define your personality. Searching for teachings and philosophies that can satisfy your needs can take some time. You need to research different belief systems to gain insights and knowledge that can help you understand the world around you.

When you discover the right path, you'll develop a keen interest in it and become eager to share it. You will be more interested in helping others learn what you already know so they can develop. These people usually become excellent teachers and can also turn to preaching to share their belief systems with others. When you share your beliefs and ideas with others, ensure you respect their freedoms.

## Capricorn Rising

Capricorn symbol.
Bruce The Deus, CC BY-SA 4.0 <https://creativecommons.org/licenses/by-sa/4.0>, via Wikimedia Commons: https://commons.wikimedia.org/wiki/File:Deus_Capricorn.png

If you are born with Capricorn Rising, you must love challenges. You can identify people who are committed to achieving their goals

The ruler of Capricorn is Saturn, which is shown through the power you have to master difficult tasks. At the same time, you will also have the patience to understand how elements like pessimism, fear, and negativity can affect your desire to reach your goals.

The qualities of your moon sign, sun sign, and house must also be considered. The time you were born determines your rising sign.

The zodiac sign which was on the horizon during the time of your birth determines your sign. Capricorn Risings are usually ambitious, but the good thing is that Saturn makes them cautious. They don't rush into trusting something before they've taken the time to understand any situation before making any big decisions. Many Capricorn risings are calculated, and they don't rush into actions that can be disappointing in the end.

Another good thing about Capricorn Rising is that they focus on their future and take actions that will lead to long-term satisfaction. They know that trust is gained over a long time and is not an overnight event. For this reason, Capricorn risings carefully choose the people they can associate with. No haters and unmotivated people are allowed in the ring of Capricorn risings. If you want to be part of them, you'd better up your game, or you will be left behind.

Individuals belonging to this group are focused on money and determined to turn their dreams into reality. With their determination, few things get in their way. They are not bothered by the opinions and feelings of other people.

The Capricorn rising people are interested in working out the value of a relationship before opening up to others. For them, it's vital to understand other people's motivations before trusting other people. If you are lucky enough to be trusted, you will become a long-term investment to these people.

### The Mindset of Capricorn Rising

The Capricorn risings are primarily concerned about money. They have realized that few things are worth sweating for besides making money. According to their doctrine, there is no need to waste energy on things they may not have in the next five years.

Capricorn energy focuses on dealing with issues that can last a long time. They first analyze the pros and cons of different situations before they involve themselves. They can drop specific actions once they suspect the end result might not be desirable. Although they can care about you or love you, they remain focused. If you are not part of them, then you are against them.

### How to Make Your Way to the Top

Material resources are your prime concern when your ascendant is Capricorn. You may be strict, stern, or serious about achieving your goals. Some people are likely to respect you for your pragmatism and capability to work hard. You will learn from your past mistakes and other people's errors and try to turn everything into an opportunity.

Capricorn risings are interested in making decisions driven by their desire to attain long-term goals in life. Many people view these individuals as practical, goal-oriented, and pragmatic. They wait for the right time to reveal surprises to their peers. You need to make efficient use of the resources you have at hand to achieve your goals. This will help you become the master of your destiny. You can achieve this by carefully planning your approach to achieve your desired goals.

You must have self-respect and treat others as you would in a team situation. If the team makes a mistake, you are likely to remember and not repeat it. However, you need to focus on the things that you already have at the moment.

### Capricorn Rising at Work

Capricorn risings are concerned with achieving their goals, which drives them to put their best efforts into whatever they are doing. They appear poised and quite solemn and serious and not the sort of people to play the fool at work. They are also quick and precise when undertaking their daily tasks. Capricorns have a gift for understanding and interpreting information quickly and easily. Other people often feel insecure when they are around the Capricorn risings because they will feel inferior.

The ascendant Capricorn is known for their determination and work ethic, so it's not surprising that this rising also has a lot of success in their careers. These ambitious individuals take their careers seriously, which is why Capricorns are often found in management roles. They're detail-oriented, strategic thinkers who take the time to plan out every step of a process before beginning it. This cautious, calculated approach makes them excellent project managers and team leaders who can see potential problems lurking around every corner. They enjoy working with facts and figures, which explains why many Capricorns choose STEM fields (science, technology, engineering, and math). They don't shy away from getting their hands dirty as an earth sign. Some common career paths for those born under the sign of the goat include architecture, accounting, civil engineering, and real estate.

### Capricorn Risings and Relationships

When in a relationship, the Capricorn risings often reveal their positive characteristics. However, they usually take some time to show themselves to their partner. They tend to lead secretive lives and avoid sharing personal information with new people. They will open up at a later stage when they gain the trust of the new person involved.

Most Capricorn risings are hesitant to allow anyone into their close social circle to protect their privacy. They will let you know their feelings if you cross their path or even warn you to mind your business. These people are easily overwhelmed by emotions when in relationships and can easily shed tears. It is vital to understand them so you know how to deal with them.

### Capricorn Rising and Love

Capricorn risings are genuine when they are in love, and they don't want a one-sided or conditional. When they love someone, there are no strings attached, and they expect the same in return. They make sure their partner is cared for, well-fed, and catered for. If you wonder whether the Capricorn rising loves you or not, this will usually answer your question - it means they don't love you or are not yet ready for you. The issue is that Capricorns cannot pretend to love someone they don't care about since they lead busy lives. If you find yourself in this situation, you should not waste your time. Instead, you should move on.

### Capricorn Rising at Home

Home is where your heart is, right? So what does that say about you if your home is a mess and all you want to do is lock yourself in your room and escape from the rest of the world? A Capricorn rising at home means you're a reserved, practical person who loves order and structure. But this doesn't mean that you don't have any fun! The key to life as a Capricorn rising at home is finding a balance between work, rest, and play.

Capricorn risings love homes with enough space to include the things they cherish, like plants, paintings, a decent dining set, and other household items. Once the Capricorn rising finds a partner, they can improve the appearance of their home. They also want room for their athletic activities. You should not be surprised to see them with a yoga mat in their home. They treat their home as a special place where they can live in peace.

**Patience and Endurance**

Ambitions may not always go your way, but they will certainly become possible depending on your approach. If you are concerned about achieving something, you should know that perseverance and endurance pay off. You can read clues from your sign to gain insight into different things you can encounter in your life. Saturn is your ruler and is responsible for teaching your life lessons and how commitment and patience can help you achieve them.

Hardships are inevitable, and they can affect your desire to achieve your goals. However, you can overcome them by reviewing your objective and respecting the laws and other forces that can affect you. You need to exercise self-discipline to get what you want. It is vital to set realistic goals to make your life easier. With Capricorn rising, you should expect to experience hardships or limitations that can affect you at each turn. However, you must be careful about believing that life must be hard.

Indeed, challenges in life are inevitable, but it does not necessarily mean they are unconquerable. Learning to appreciate challenging work can set you apart from other people who subject themselves to fate. You need to put your ambitions into perspective and make sure your goals are achievable.

**Pleasures of Life**

Life is not only about discipline and hard work. You also need to recognize that you need to take time to relax and enjoy your life. Sensual pleasure is an integral component of our lives, so you should not deprive yourself of happiness and other activities that can make you relax. Self-repression can negatively impact your goals, especially if you are over-ambitious.

If you are responsive, this ascendant helps you work hard to achieve the goals you want. The best partner is someone who understands your aspirations and goals and supports you in achieving them. You also need to avoid things that can impede the pursuit of your goals. Follow the rules and regulations to avoid disappointment. In whatever you pursue, remember this sign is associated with earthly pleasures.

With Capricorn rising, balancing the desire to achieve your goals and downtime is essential; this also helps you recognize your capabilities and what you can achieve. Make sure you pursue happiness since it is good for your social well-being. Do not focus on material things alone since there are more things to life.

In this chapter, we explained the characteristics of people with Sagittarius rising and Capricorn rising signs, their qualities, and what makes them different from others. The next chapter focuses on Aquarius rising and Pisces rising.

# Chapter 9: Aquarius Rising and Pisces Rising

In this chapter, we focus on Aquarius rising and Pisces rising signs. We explain different traits that characterize the people who belong to these rising signs. We'll highlight the characteristics that make these people who they are and what motivates their lives.

Aquarius rising and Pisces rising are two of the most challenging ascendants to have. With Aquarius as your rising sign, you'll be forever exploring new ideas and concepts and your unique identity. You may feel like an outsider for much of your life because you don't necessarily fit in with others around you. Similarly, with Pisces rising, you'll almost always feel misunderstood by those around you since they simply won't understand the way you think or see the world. Both of these ascendants require a lot of alone time, and a trusted few who can see past their oddities and get to know them at their core. Here we explore more about Aquarius rising vs. Pisces rising and how they affect your personality and outlook on life:

# Aquarius Rising

Aquarius symbol.
*Bruce The Deus, CC BY-SA 4.0 <https://creativecommons.org/licenses/by-sa/4.0>, via Wikimedia Commons: https://commons.wikimedia.org/wiki/File:Deus_Aquarius.png*

Many years ago, people believed Saturn ruled Aquarius, but after recent research, it is agreed that Uranus now rules it. Aquarius has a dark history which means it is a sign not to play around with. Uranus is regarded as a planet of rebellion and chaos, and this extends to people who belong to Aquarius rising. They often experience a feeling of confusion and loss.

Therefore, the greater purpose of Aquarius rinsing's existence is mainly concerned with maintaining order. They also try to make as much sense to the world as possible. They will fight to protect their community because it is one of their greatest possessions. They also want peace so they can follow their interests.

## The Mindset of Aquarius Rising

Aquarius risings trust their instincts, and they have an outstanding mindset. If they believe something to be true, they will follow their minds. Another notable characteristic about Aquarius risings is that if they oppose a motion, they will go in the opposite direction from other people. Like Aquarius suns, the Aquarius risings believe they are superior to everyone else.

Aquarius risings who are keen to learn new things can benefit by acknowledging their mistakes. This mindset promotes learning and knowledge acquisition, unlike people who mistakenly think they are always right. The water bearer represents Aquarius and reflects the rising's everyday life. They are always available to give a hand to the people they love and take their time to share anything that may affect their peers.

Aquarius rising people are reserved and often try to distance themselves from others as being the source of entertainment is stressful. They understand that one needs to be committed to being available to everyone. They believe that if you make a promise, you should keep it. When the Aquarius risings feel they no longer want to hang out with a certain group of people, they will fade away. They usually have good reasons for that kind of behavior.

Aquarius risings feel they have so many responsibilities they don't have time to attend to everyone. They also view other people who may not add value to their lives as vampires. However, these people have exceptional traits that make them excellent companions. For instance, if you intend to start a project, you can get inspiration from them to achieve your desired goals.

**Aquarius Rising and Work**

Individuals who belong to Aquarius rising signs are very hard workers and are determined to achieve all their goals. Once they commit themselves to a particular mission, they ensure it is accomplished. They are committed to achieving their mission instead of focusing on individuals. They know that people are not perfect and can make mistakes, which is why they commit themselves to the project, not the team members. Goal attainment is the main focus, which makes the Aquarius Risings unique from other groups in different societies.

They are concerned about how to reach structural equity, and they are leaders who stand by their beliefs. They do not suffer fools lightly and will walk away from nonsense if they get bored or people question their ideas. The Aquarius risings believe that individuals should trust their own instincts but respect the community.

Aquarius risings are excellent water bearers who become great professionals because of their outstanding community organizing skills. Their core values are focused on helping marginalized people and standing up for the rights of the less privileged members of society. They want to create a place where everyone can enjoy life and pursue their goals.

Aquarius risings always think of the bigger picture and want to reach bigger goals first. However, this does not necessarily mean they are obsessed with work. They also have other important things they want to achieve in their lives. This helps them structure their work and have a total commitment to any career path they are involved in. They believe a career is part of their identity. The good thing about Aquarians is that they have an appealing passionate nature that can motivate people to love their careers and anything they do for the benefit of others.

**Relationships and Aquarius Rising**

There is often a misconception that their Aquarius energy does not produce a perfect partner. However, if you believe this, you might be the one on the wrong side. Aquarius risings have great respect for their relationships, love, and friendship. They'll try to defend the people they love and do everything to understand their partners. They freely celebrate the achievements of their partners. They relish the company of others.

Aquarius risings are fun, easy-going, and light-hearted people. If they are in a relationship that gives them freedom and independence, they can thrive in whatever they are doing. If they seem to be down, this may be caused by pressure. So if you're in a relationship with one, give your partner plenty of space and don't take everything they say seriously.

To enjoy the best relationship with an Aquarius rising, you should focus on what you can give or do to make your partner happy. You should not always expect to get something from the person you love. Aquarius risings admire famous people, artists, and performers. They also have extensive networks that help them achieve their goals. The advantage of a strong network is to make tasks easier. Therefore, if you want to create links with famous people, ask an Aquarius rising to help you achieve your goal. They will probably know several people who are ready to volunteer their time for the benefit of other individuals.

**Aquarius Rising and Love**

Aquarius Risings are inquisitive and enjoy experimenting with different things to get answers to different problems. They are usually composed, and you can easily see if they are flirting. Signs like raised eyebrows and other facial expressions can tell you they are enjoying themselves.

They treat love as a fun experience, and they will develop interest along the way. Aquarius risings take their time to understand the person they are interested in. For instance, they will ask for personal details like hobbies, interests, and how you see different things in relationships. Your answers will determine if they feel you are the one they want to have a relationship with and how you'll be as a partner. If you feel you are under a microscope or are in an interrogation, don't worry, it's just Aquarius checking your character so they don't waste anyone's time in a dead-end relationship.

You will be very lucky to enter into a relationship with an Aquarius rising because they are genuine people. They will show their true personality if they know they can trust you. These are wonderful people who are easy to go along with.

If you want the Aquarius partner to show you love, always be honest and never deceitful – that will mean certain death to your relationship. They will drop you instantly if they feel they are being trifled with and messed around. Equally, don't play mind games with them, you won't win, and you'll risk a wonderful relationship.

**Aquarius Rising and Home**

Aquarius Risings prefer to live in comfortable homes where they can prepare their favorite dishes and listen to the best music. They treat the home as the best place to be, so they adorn it with the best things they can afford to make their lifestyle what they want it to be. However, they do not believe in spectacular mansions but in special places that make them feel like kings or queens.

Aquarius risings decorate their homes with plants, aquariums, and unique furniture. They incorporate different things that depict life in their homes. They create plenty of natural arrangements in their homes to show how they value nature. You should not be surprised to find that each room has a unique plant, and this is when you will discover that Aquarius risings love weird and strange things.

Once they choose a way of life, they do not backtrack and always find a way to their luxury. They are particular about their comfort and are not wasteful people. Additionally, they always try to find the means to perfect their art of living using the resources available to enjoy life to the fullest.

# Pisces Rising

Pisces symbol.
*Bruce The Deus, CC BY-SA 4.0 <https://creativecommons.org/licenses/by-sa/4.0>, via Wikimedia Commons: https://commons.wikimedia.org/wiki/File:Deus_Pisces.png*

Your outer layer is the rising sign that determines how you appear to others. People who belong to Pisces often feel detached when young, but what they should know is that life is multi-dimensional. The Pisces rising is receptive, kind, and at times lost-looking.

Their persona may seem changeable, and if you belong to this category, you can morph into different masks to match the existing company. You are a chameleon; you can align your personality to match those around you. However, stronger personalities can easily overwhelm you. So you must be careful who you choose to be around you.

You thrive when you surround yourself with supportive friends who share your interests and vision. Pisces rising people can use their imagination and are talented in using symbols, sounds, and movement to reflect life. The most common ways of expressing themselves are through music, drama, dance, and visual arts. When Pisces is your rising sign, Neptune is the ruler of your chart.

### Open Borders

Pisces rising people are compassionate and gather lost people and stray animals. However, you may be vulnerable to people who don't share your sentiments and are easily taken advantage of.

When they look at you, they see potential prey. If you fail to pair critical thinking with your intuition, you may become a victim.

While you can lose yourself easily, you need to learn life lessons to set clear boundaries that will keep you away from people who may take advantage of you. In some cases, you may be on the wrong side by following the crowd, even if you see that it will be destructive. There are often sad stories of naïve of people who followed blindly and ended up in the deep end.

If you are Pisces rising, you are compassionate even about the dark forces among us. However, there is the risk of throwing yourself in harm's way. If you are intuitive, you can use that to save your life. This can only be possible if you heed your intuition. You need to take your time to study the people around you before you blindly trust them and bring them into your life. The more you observe and learn about people, the more confidence you will get in your decision-making about them, and the fewer mistakes you'll make by trusting the wrong people

In some cases, it is good for your soul to be alone. Staying away from people who may be a bad influence in your life can save you from many things. For instance, you may end up falling into the trap of addiction if you associate with bad company. This will affect your thinking and lead to bad decisions that can impact your life and overall well-being.

### Mystic Attitude

The rising sign influences the way you move into the world. With Pisces rising, you are accustomed to things like dreams, good luck, and symbolic language. Too much socializing can overwhelm you, and enough time alone can be restorative. It is crucial to take some time to do the things you love most, like watching movies, reading books, or playing music. You also need to give yourself free time when you are not doing anything. When your mind is clear and you know what you want in life, you will grow strong.

### Pisces Rising Mannerism and Appearance

People with Pisces rising are generally accommodative, kind, and prone to be dreamers. Most of them are soft and appear timid. They often present themselves in such a way that they can't cope with the struggles of the world and daily life because they seem weak. However, these are all mannerisms. Pisces rising mannerisms can be described as gentle, spiritual, sacrificial, dreamy, approachable, selfless, and empathetic.

Pisces Risings are compassionate and sensitive to others, but they always desire to escape reality. They often achieve this by turning to things like music, alcohol, drugs, or art.

### Personality

The people with a Pisces ascendant behave like chameleons because they always change their personalities to adapt to different environments around them. However, few people realize this as they hide it so well. While most people will see the Pisces zodiac sign as being shy or timid, those with the Pisces personality are anything but. These individuals are incredibly intuitive and sensitive, which allows them to see past the surface of things. They're also incredibly compassionate and selfless, willing to give without expecting anything in return quite often.

### High on Life

Pisces rising individuals appear to be on top of situations, which can be contagious. They want to create a rosy worldview and refuse to see its ugliness which makes them often live in fantasy. Because they're so giving, many assume that Pisces rising don't have a backbone or any real strength of character, but this couldn't be further from the truth. They have a quiet strength and courage that few other people can match. They know who they are and what they stand for and have no fear about going after what they want or speaking the truth as they see it. When you're on top of the world because you're so confident in who you are as a person and what you stand for as an individual, that's being high on life as a Pisces!

### Depths of Despair

The Pisces Rising people are not always stable as ups and downs characterize their lives. Although they may have high hopes in life, they are quickly shattered if they fail to achieve their desired goals. As a result, they will turn to drugs and substances to drown their sorrows. In some cases, despair and loneliness can lead to suicide if it's left uncontrolled.

### Pisces Rising and Relationships

The people with Pisces Rising are passive in a relationship, and they expect their partner to play the dominant active role. They idealize their partners and offer selfless love. These people are romantic and try to create emotional ties with their partners. However, they will suffer a disproportionate setback when the lover fails to live up to their expectations.

### Pisces Rising Women, Men, and Children

Pisces rising women are attractive and very feminine. They also have several qualities that make them adorable. They love fashion and other things that can enhance their beauty.

Men with Pisces rising are charismatic, and they have big dreams. They are interested in pursuing their goals and want to keep them secret. They want their freedom and don't want people to interfere with their aspirations. In other words, they must be understood and encouraged to follow their dreams.

Children with Pisces rising are sensitive and delicate. They are loving, sweet, gentle, and cooperative such that their parents often find it difficult to believe that their children can do anything wrong. However, parents often fail to provide proper guidance to their children because they are overprotective. The kids often get away with anything since they can create convincing fairy tales when they are suspected of wrongdoing. Pisces rising kids need to be closely monitored; otherwise, they can grow up to be spoiled adults.

### Hidden Talent

People with Pisces rising have hidden artistic talent. They can become a writer, musician, a dancer, an actor, or any other type of creative person. However, it is not easy to have Pisces on the ascendant. Great art comes from dedication and commitment.

In this chapter, we explained the traits of people with Aquarius rising and Pisces rising. The Aquarius rising people are unique and believe in their instincts and always think they are right. Pisces rising people are compassionate and possess a great love for others.

# Chapter 10: A Guide to Embrace Your Rising Sign

The subject of astrology is fascinating to many people. And many more are intrigued by the discoveries that can be made by looking further into the subject. While the concepts of the rising sign have existed for thousands of years, a lot of what was once known has now been lost. But the primary concepts continue to exist along with unique interpretations.

When you learn how your rising sign influences different parts of your life and what the implications are, it becomes much less surprising when things happen the way they do. You are likely to be more focused, independent, and open-minded than others. In many cultures worldwide, people celebrate this illuminating aspect of astrology by taking an active role in realizing their full potential and developing their particular gifts.

The essence of such knowledge is an occasion for celebration. It brings a sense of empowerment and hopes to everyone. However, as any good astrologist and actualized person knows, *knowledge is always a caveat.* Certainly, you can stop your rune journey at this point and enjoy what you have learned and what you have crafted so far. There is still so much to learn if you want to progress further. Having a collection of runes isn't enough. You must understand how to handle your rising sign to take full advantage of your new status.

The rest of this chapter will provide you with information about how to embrace your rising sign and those of others. We will also cover how you can learn more about the craft and why it is essential to get the most out of this aspect of astrology and faith. Because when you realize the wealth of opportunities and benefits that your rising sign can bring, you will wonder how you ever lived with it.

## Understand Rising Signs

Over time, we have become increasingly aware of the fact that there are thousands of other people out there who share the same interests and experiences. In response to this, individuals have found ways to reach out to one another to strengthen their sense of belonging. Those with a particular penchant for identifying with the rising signs can find solace in identifying as such and socializing with others who feel the same. Becoming involved in the world of astrology is an excellent way to strengthen one's identity while meeting new people and broadening one's horizons. However, this comes with its own unique challenges and pitfalls. The world of astrology is not everyone's cup of tea — those who identify as part of this subculture often face numerous misconceptions, difficulties integrating – and even discrimination, at times, because of it.

If you are aware and interested in learning more about astrology, you know that it is not something that simply rolls out of the heavens and aligns with positive influences in your life. To embrace astrology, you must work at it and understand the concepts behind it. To succeed, you must be willing to learn about the subject, see how it can support your thinking, and act based on what you learn.

For example, let's say you are a huge basketball fan and are excited about the upcoming season. However, every year your team misses the playoffs. What if there was another way to look at your season that doesn't focus on whether or not they will make the playoffs? What if you could look at it as an opportunity for growth instead of a time when everything goes wrong? Incorporating the rising signs into your life could be one of the best things you do for yourself.

### Embrace the Magnitude

Astrology is often viewed as something mystical and unapproachable. However, this isn't the case. In fact, many people worldwide have a great love for astrology and what it has to offer. Many people are put off by the idea of exploring their own rising sign or horoscope because they think it sounds strange and creepy. However, being interested in your own personal traits is nothing weird or abnormal. And that's exactly why you should embrace astrology if you haven't already! Learning more about your zodiac sign can actually be really beneficial, especially when you combine it with other self-improvement techniques such as meditation and mindfulness.

Most people who enter into more advanced forms of astrology soon realize that astrology is not just about their Sun sign or the 12 signs but also about planets, houses, and birth information. It's amazing to know that the different signs of the zodiac can be aligned in different places in the sky, making them relevant to life's obstacles and offerings.

Everything is contained within your birth chart. Here you will find out what has been cast since the moment you were born. So, the time, date, and location of birth are necessary to generate an appropriate and comprehensive birth chart. This is at least a starting point.

You will find it confusing the first time you see one because when you learn astrology, you're essentially learning a new language. The symbols and glyph characters in this language will initially be unfamiliar to you.

Astrology is an ancient science that explores the connection between human and celestial bodies. It can be hard to understand something so abstract and mysterious, especially when you're first learning about it. But with time and practice, you'll learn to embrace astrology as another part of your life.

### Never Stop Learning

To learn astrology, there are a few things you need to do. Despite their simplicity, each method can take a lot of time and energy, depending on how committed you are. You'll need to talk, study, practice, and read astrology and rising signs as much as

possible.
- Online
- Books
- Websites
- eBooks
- Blogs
- Social Media
- Magazines

Astrology is an art, science, and philosophy all in one. Learning about astrology will help you gain a deeper understanding of the universe and your own life. The more you know about astrology, the more impressive your readings will be! Astrology is a vast and expansive field that can take an entire lifetime to fully understand. Even the most knowledgeable astrologers continue to learn more about their craft and its origins daily. And while there is no wrong way to learn astrology, certain methods are more beneficial than others. The best way to advance your knowledge of astrology is by reading books, taking classes or workshops, and practicing regularly. Astrologers have been writing books for centuries, and many of them can still be purchased today, either as print books or as eBooks. There are many good beginner astrology guides out there, so a good look around the internet, and you'll be able to pick up a couple of them.

**Create a To-Do List**

In this subsequent section, we will cover some ways to bring Norse magic into your life if you have no knowledge of astrology and the rising signs.

Here are some things you can do to learn more:

- Find an online course or meet with someone in person to receive formal training
- Read journals, blogs, books, and websites
- Search Google, Meetup.com, or NCGR (National Council for Geocosmic Research) for local groups
- Check out any astrology pages on social media (Reddit is

best)
- Double-check your birth time
- Get a copy of or make your own birth chart
- Make your own or buy some runes
- Learn the symbols for the zodiac signs, planets, houses, etc.
- Take advantage of free online resources, such as blogs, websites, podcasts, YouTube, and Reddit
- If there are no meet-up groups in your area, then start your own
- The Astrology Dictionary
- Take a look at the birth charts of your friends, family, and famous people (you can find birth data online for many celebrities)
- Online or locally, you can take an astrology course
- Join an astrological organization and attend one of their conferences

## Make Use of Online Sources

This is a no-brainer, but because knowledge of rising signs isn't usual and easy to find, you may feel alone in your new passion. But this couldn't be further from the truth. So, make use of free resources online. You can use them for simple things like learning the symbols for the signs, planets, and their meaning. Imagine if the runes' origin and power were documented in the way we document things today; online.

The internet is full of free resources. There is almost no end to it all. And the amount of free, quality information means there's no reason for small-budget enthusiasts not to study the craft. Look for the following:

- Astrology blogs and websites.
- PDFs of free astrological texts and other related things
- Podcasts and free episodes on Audible or Spotify
- YouTube has a wealth of information on all aspects of Norse magic, from techniques to topics

## Talk to Others

You need to talk to other people. Communication is an underestimated learning tool. We need to interact with other people about the topic and language, the rising signs, astrology in general, as well as the faith aspects of it. Looking up local astrological groups on the web is important if you are considering meeting up with other astrology lovers. You can usually find many individuals around you looking for companionship in their interest in astrology, even if it is new to you. If you take a look, you may be able to locate a group to meet up with in person; if not, there are plenty of excellent online groups where people are very friendly and helpful.

## Become a Student

One of the greatest things you can do is to take a structured course. However, people who start studying astrology don't realize that astrology becomes a lifelong job, passion, or interest for most people. It's very important, therefore, to obtain a solid base, a great foundation, or some great grounding in the basics if you can learn from a teacher or teachers.

Learning through a course with an astrologer will give you a great foundation.
https://unsplash.com/photos/jCIMcOpFHig?utm_source=unsplash&utm_medium=referral&utm_content=creditShareLink

Astrology is too vast a subject for one teacher to teach you everything you need to know. It's also too big a subject for one person to study alone. But being introduced to astrology by an astrologer will give you the foundation you need for the rest of your life. After this time, you can begin attending astrology conferences or dedicating yourself to a certain subfield, as long as you can speak the language.

**Keep Your Feet on the Ground**

Everything about astrology is about understanding yourself and the forces of nature. From the moment we are born, we can see our star charts and know where our path will take us in the future. Astrological knowledge is, however, much more than knowing our zodiac signs. It is about understanding yourself and how your personality aligns with nature's laws.

It can get very exciting when you finally meet someone who is on the same page as you. You may be shocked to learn that professional or long-term rising sign enthusiasts are not attracted to reading other people's birth charts or asking for readings, for example, at conferences. And in online forums, it is more pronounced. For example, this occurs if there is a new astrology forum, and a new astrologer appears and tries to get people to read their charts. Sometimes it is considered a faux pas when people only want to ask other people about their birth charts. However, astrologers will often ask each other about placements in their birth charts to get to know another person. So, someone may initiate a conversation, but generally, it's better to join in discussions that have already been started.

Be wary of asking other people astrological questions, and don't constantly bring up your own chart to generate discussion. Instead, offer to read other people's charts as a way to practice your skills. Not only will you learn more, but it will be a great way to interact with others.

The key to interacting with other astrologers is understanding the community's social norms. A professional astrologer usually focuses on their profession, so they don't necessarily read charts all the time. They don't just throw out statements about a person's life when a stranger pulls out a chart.

People who start astrology are either looking for information about themselves or want to learn more about the art. Therefore, you should think about your motivation. And it's okay to want to learn about yourself. We are curious creatures, after all. And if you want to learn about astrology itself, then you might go about it in a slightly different way.

### Study the Rising Sign of Others

Speaking of reading birth charts, studying your own chart is not enough to learn astrology. You must also study other people's charts and transits as well. Even though your primary focus in astrology is likely to be you and your own life, one of the most entertaining things you can do is to use it to learn about the lives of others.

Study the charts of your friends, family members, or even famous people and others you are interested in to look for commonalities. Examine the chart itself or the data to determine how the locations of the stars in the chart are related to different life events and circumstances. You can study the positions of the Sun or other planets on the same day as an important life event to learn more about the person and discover how they are the way they are. Start studying the charts of other people and the planets' positions, and then apply the same process to your own chart.

Another thing you could try is comparing the birth charts of two people to see how they interact, even if you're not trying to determine their compatibility. You can also see whether the chart shows a connection between the two. For example, if you look at a composite birth chart (an advanced form of astrology) of a couple, you can see whether they are really connected.

It is when you start seeing other people's charts that you realize how diverse the study of astrology study really is. By understanding how much you can learn about other people by reading their birth charts, and other applications, you can see how ingrained it is in life exploration and personality.

### Find Solace in a Professional

You will be eager to start learning as soon as you receive your first charms, runes, and birth chart. It might be worth your while investing in a reading with a well-established astrologer. Having the opportunity to sit down with a professional to discuss your chart can be one of the most valuable things a student can do for themselves. As a result, you will get so much out of it that is relevant, and it will be as if you are having a one-on-one tutoring session. Astrology is a great way to improve your understanding of human nature and provide insight into how people are likely to respond to various events or activities. If you're considering a career in astrology, it could be the perfect opportunity for you! Astrology professionals study the movement of celestial bodies and their impact on human behavior and affairs. Astrologers use knowledge of astronomy, the positions of planets and other stars, and their effect on individuals to better understand their client's life circumstances. These professionals may work directly with clients or in another capacity, such as within research organizations or the wider community. A career in astrology may also involve teaching students about astrological concepts and principles as part of a broader curriculum that includes other areas of astronomy.

### Learn the Craft

Get started learning the zodiac signs, the planets, and the aspects of the chart by learning their symbolic representations. It has its own alphabet, representing planets and zodiac signs. This is your starting point.

The birth chart is a rich piece of information and insight, but you can only get into it if you understand the symbols. The best way to do this is memorization. Once you have these down, you'll never forget them. It will then become like a second language to you. Once memorized, you will know what Scorpio in Jupiter looks like just by identifying the symbol for Jupiter and identifying the symbol for Scorpio in the birth chart. You can understand specific placements in your birth chart and other charts as soon as you understand this.

When you are learning astrology, the emphasis is on keeping your eyes and ears open, as much as on learning the theory. This is because you are learning astrology on two levels: the theory or the way it manifests and how to add depth to your knowledge. For instance, if you want to learn astrology, you must first acquire a book on the subject, but reading and absorbing the book can also teach you a lot about the craft.

For example, knowing how to observe is a big part of learning, and astrology, in particular. Let's say you want to understand the houses better. So, you begin by tracking the sun or the moon through the houses. But, if you observe correctly, you will notice how the moon changes every couple of days. So will the outcome.

And if you track the Sun through the houses, you'll notice how topics are repeated every time the Moon is in the seventh house. You can chart the positions of the planets and the Moon to track their movements through the twelve houses of the zodiac, or you may track the Sun through the houses to see if the planets influence an aspect of your life. This observational method is rich in how it enhances your knowledge and learning.

Many things can help you embrace your rising sign and get the most out of this special element in your life. In some cases, it might just be as simple as realizing that you have a different view of the world when compared with other people. However, as with anything, you should use your rising sign to your advantage. There are various ways to do so, including learning more about other cultures and how their beliefs differ from yours. Be willing to try new things, but always be willing to stick to your guns when you do. Also, don't forget that you have very little control over what your rising sign shows you. This is just one of the many things the stars have aligned for you. So, make the most of it, and however you accept your current situation, you will likely find more peace than you have experienced in the past.

Learning about your rising sign is a process of discovery. As you journey through, you will learn more about yourself. You will also learn more about what's possible for you in the future and gain a deeper understanding of the general patterns that have impacted your life so far.

The rising sign will always be there. It is a core aspect of the astrological nature of each person. And it is a powerful influence on growth and change. You must be willing to explore and discover your rising sign, its meaning, and how it can benefit your life. The more you know about it, the more you will be able to appreciate its value, and the more likely you will be able to take advantage of it.

# Conclusion

The rising sign is one of the most important astrological aspects that affects your natal chart readings. The rising sign is specific to everyone and decides their ruling planet. It basically refers to the zodiac sign that was rising on the eastern horizon at the time of someone's birth. This zodiac sign changes every two hours, and to identify your rising sign, you need to know the exact time of your birth.

It reveals the significant sides of your personality. While many think these traits reflect your outer persona, they are intrinsic quirks and traits directly associated with your real self. The rising sign can be identified from your natal chart, and after reading the birth chart guide chapter, there should be a straightforward interpretation of your chart, ascendant and ruling planets.

Each chapter looked deeply into the traits, patterns, and themes associated with the rising signs. So, there should be no confusion about the characteristics of each rising sign, whether it's Aries, Taurus, Gemini, Cancer, Leo, Virgo, Libra, Scorpio, Sagittarius, Capricorn, Aquarius, or Pisces. The best part about these chapters? They go into detail about the rising sign's personality, mindset, work behavior, how they deal with relationships, love, and friendships, and how they treat their family.

This in-depth explanation makes it easy for you to understand your ascendant and also makes it easier for you to embrace it. Once you understand your strengths and weaknesses, nothing can stop you from loving yourself and changing yourself for the better.

# Here's another book by Silvia Hill that you might like

# Free Bonus from Silvia Hill available for limited time

Hi Spirituality Lovers!

My name is Silvia Hill, and first off, I want to THANK YOU for reading my book.

Now you have a chance to join my exclusive spirituality email list so you can get the ebooks below for free as well as the potential to get more spirituality ebooks for free! Simply click the link below to join.

P.S. Remember that it's 100% free to join the list.

### ~~$27~~ FREE BONUSES

- 9 Types of Spirit Guides and How to Connect to Them
- How to Develop Your Intuition: 7 Secrets for Psychic Development and Tarot Reading
- Tarot Reading Secrets for Love, Career, and General Messages

Access your free bonuses here
https://livetolearn.lpages.co/rising-signs-paperback/

# References

Coffey, J. (2009, December 27). Celestial Body. Universe Today. https://www.universetoday.com/48671/celestial-body/

Farnell, K. (2020). The man behind the horoscope column: R H Naylor. Astrology Quarterly. https://www.academia.edu/49600969/The_man_behind_the_horoscope_column_R_H_Naylor

Hall, M. (2011, November 12). Chart elements: Parts of the astrological birth chart. LiveAbout. https://www.liveabout.com/chart-parts-and-points-207194

Roberts, S. (2018, October 7). Babylonian astrology: How Mesopotamian priests influenced your horoscope. Ancient Origins. https://www.ancient-origins.net/history-ancient-traditions/babylonian-astrology-0010806

The Editors of Encyclopedia Britannica. (2021). astrology summary. In Encyclopedia Britannica.

We'Moon. (n.d.). What Sign is the Moon in, What is My Moon Sign, and What Does it all Mean? We'Moon. https://wemoon.ws/blogs/journey-into-astrology/what-sign-is-the-moon-in-and-what-does-that-mean

William Lilly (Lilly, William, 1602-1681). (n.d.). Upenn.edu. http://onlinebooks.library.upenn.edu/webbin/book/lookupname?key=Lilly%2C%20William%2C%201602%2D1681

Almanac.com homepage. (n.d.). Almanac.com. https://www.almanac.com/

Astrology Zodiac Signs. (n.d.). 12 astrology zodiac signs dates, meanings, and compatibility. Astrology-zodiac-signs.com. https://www.astrology-zodiac-signs.com/

Morin, A. (2012, October 12). Find out what a glyph is in archeology, language, and typography. ThoughtCo. https://www.thoughtco.com/what-is-a-glyph-2086584

Planets. (n.d.). NASA Solar System Exploration https://solarsystem.nasa.gov/planets/overview/

Beusman, C. (2018, October 17). Astrology is hard, even if it's fake. The New York Times. https://www.nytimes.com/2018/10/17/style/astrology-exam.html

Planets. (n.d.). Astrology.com. https://www.astrology.com/planets

Thomas, K. (2021, November 5). A guide to the planets in astrology and what they each represent. New York Post. https://nypost.com/article/astrology-planets-meaning/

Aries Ascendant / Rising Sign. (2015, April 21). Cafeastrology.com. https://cafeastrology.com/aries_ascendantrisingsign.html

Denise. (2018, November 9). Aries Rising: The influence of Aries Ascendant on personality. I.TheHoroscope.Co. https://i.thehoroscope.co/aries-rising-the-influence-of-aries-ascendant-on-personality/

Hall, M. (2009, May 23). Learn the easiest way to interpret a Taurus Rising birth chart. LiveAbout. https://www.liveabout.com/taurus-rising-rising-signs-207237

Holmes, M. (2022a, January 28). All the details on what Aries risings are *really* like. Cosmopolitan. https://www.cosmopolitan.com/lifestyle/a35293409/aries-rising/

Holmes, M. (2022b, March 8). If you're a Taurus Rising, we know what you're *really* like. Cosmopolitan. https://www.cosmopolitan.com/lifestyle/a35568032/taurus-rising/

Maffucci, S. (2022, May 18). What it means if you have Taurus rising as your ascendant sign. YourTango. https://www.yourtango.com/zodiac/taurus-rising-sign-ascendant

More on Taurus Ascendant, rising sign. (2015, April 18). Cafeastrology.com; Cafe Astrology .com. https://cafeastrology.com/taurus_ascendantrisingsign.html

Nunes, D. (2022, May 12). What it means if you have Aries rising as your Ascendant sign. YourTango. https://www.yourtango.com/zodiac/aries-rising-sign-ascendant

Sylvester, M. (2022, April 16). Aries rising sign: How it affects your personality & love life. Elite Daily. https://www.elitedaily.com/lifestyle/aries-rising-sign-personality-love-life

Sylvester, M. (2022, April 16). Cancer Rising Sign: How It Affects Your Personality & Love Life. Elite Daily. https://www.elitedaily.com/lifestyle/aries-rising-sign-personality-love-life

Sylvester, M. (2022, July 9). Gemini Rising Sign: How It Affects Your Personality & Love Life. Elite Daily. https://www.elitedaily.com/lifestyle/cancer-rising-sign-personality-love-life

Denise. (2018, November 9). Gemini Rising: The Influence of Gemini Ascendant on Personality. I.TheHoroscope.Co. https://i.thehoroscope.co/gemini-rising-the-influence-of-gemini-ascendant-on-personality

www.ingramcontent.com/pod-product-compliance
Lightning Source LLC
Chambersburg PA
CBHW070338010526
44107CB00004B/540